Contents

For my husband,

who has unquestioning faith in my abilities,
and for my parents, without whom,
I would not be a writer.

1
Two Lines to a Stick

When Husband and I decided to get married, we were told we'd spend so much time together that finding a hobby would be beneficial. Loads of thought and three games of *Rock, Paper, Scissors* later, he and I came to the conclusion that underwater basket weaving was too time consuming, so we decided on children instead. That was the reason I'd been sitting in the bathroom for almost a half an hour when I heard my love call up the stairs.

"You all right in there?"

"Yeah, just thinking."

"In the bathroom?"

I turned the little cardboard box over in my hands and shouted at the closed door, "All the greats do their thinking in the bathroom. The screenplay for *Glitter* didn't write itself, you know." Holding the stick a safe distance away, I shook it and ignored my soul mate's guttural calls. No change.

Disbelief prompted me to set down my *Calvin and*

Hobbes and evaluate the situation. Pants around ankles, left hand braced against the sink, I squinted at my future, which, at first glance, had been yellow and splotchy. A second glance confirmed it was not only yellow, but also had little, pink marks floating in it. I looked back at Calvin and Hobbes. "You guys keep building that fort and teaching cleverly veiled life lessons. I've got to go reassess my existence up to this point."

I continued sitting on my warm, porcelain throne and stared at the wall. The key was to not move. If I moved, time would progress and my belly would get bigger, pants tighter. That, and we were dangerously close to being out of toilet paper. With only one jagged square left, I evaluated the technique needed to fold it to the proper dimensions for splatter resistance and sufficient cleaning circumference. Perhaps an origami swan or elegant crane? Surely the swan was nature's more absorbent bird.

When the standard amount of time for such an excursion had long passed, and after Husband may have had cause to wonder if I'd died of a hernia or started watching every season of *Lost* over again, I inched my way off the toilet and, oh so carefully, slid my pants back on. I had to be careful. Someone depended on me. If I got all crazy and started jerking pants on all willy-nilly, what could that do to a baby? A little person was nestling in at that precise moment, getting comfy in my uterus, not appreciating my uncoordinated dressing abilities. It occurred to me that there was probably a whole community of people out in the world whose right arms were shorter than their left, all because their mothers couldn't figure out how to put their pants on correctly.

I could see the Matt Lauer interview: "And why do the doctors think your arms came out uneven?"

"My pregnant mother did an unexpected downward dog while trying to zip her American Eagle hip-huggers and I got caught in the malaise of un-toned abs and ill-fitting sale denim."

"That sounds awful."

"It was, Matt. The woman still doesn't know how to move cautiously when she's trying to retrieve stray Skittles from under the refrigerator. It's like watching a mongoose hunt small woodland creatures in the night."

As I continued to stare at the wall, I realized I was slowly losing it, but the craziness felt really good, like the velour track suit I'd bought in college. So wrong, but so right. So Jenny From the Block, yet so Bennifer.

Taking a timeout and breathing would've been wise, but I'd already taken the dive, head-first, into the shallow pool of insane detective mode. What were they always saying on *CSI*? Evidence, I needed lots and lots of evidence. I needed more white plastic sticks to wet on before I jumped to conclusions. David Caruso had done that in an episode. Which reminded me; I probably needed a pair of Aviators to deliver the news to friends and family.

More sticks equaled keys. Keys that one used to do what? Oh, right, start the car. What was a car? Oh yeah, in the garage. Needed to get to the garage. I quietly opened the bathroom door, padded down the stairs, and located the metal thing responsible for starting my vehicle.

"Honey? Honey, you goin' out?"

I stopped. "Yeah," I managed.

"Cool. Grab some Coke while you're out?"

My hand found the door handle. "Sure. Like, the drink?"

"Umm, yeah. Like, in the case."

I closed my eyes and bit my lip. "Yeah. I mean, that would be silly if you meant crack cocaine. Taking up a hard-core illegal habit on a Saturday when you could just run down to the gas station sounds like a lot of extra work. Everyone knows you only make decisions that ruin your life on a Monday, so you can use a sick day."

"You all right?"

"Yep, just glad we're both clear I'm simply going to the gas station and not bringing back two kilos of the White Mosquito."

Keys shaking in my hand, I wobbled all the way to my little white sports car, opened the door, and slipped inside.

"Zombie! Zooooooombie!" Many people are unaware, but screaming the Cranberries at the top of one's lungs is extremely therapeutic. (Faux Irish yodeling also clears regularity problems right up.) My first choice of therapy would've been doing the Electric Slide in my underwear after five gin and tonics, but I didn't have the room to dance, and hadn't looked up whether babies liked gin or not. Deciding to err on the side of caution seemed wise. Instead, I channeled Dolores O'Riordan, pretended I could effortlessly hit a high C, understood the suffering of my ancestors, and floored it down the street. The storm of yodeling was quelled only by finding a parking spot at the drug store and tearing through the doors in search of the magical wands that would point me to my destiny.

Two. Three. Four. Not understanding why someone hadn't figured out how to put twenty to a package, I tried not to look frustrated when I dumped my pile of boxes on the counter. "It's for my friend. For me. For my best friend, which is me, because I can't make friends due to spontaneous lying and verbal incontinence."

While I dug for my debit card, I could feel the heat of judgment radiating off the sales lady. I did my best to swipe my card with my ring hand.

See that, lady? It's legit. If you wanna give someone a dirty look, here's my address. Husband's parked on the couch, and the only one you should be eyeing right now. Just don't have a drink with him. He'll start pawing you and telling you your hair looks soooo good but would look better without pants on.

The drive back played out pretty much like the journey to the store. This time, I backed Mariah Carey while she sang "Forever." Normally, she and I would take turns throwing three-part harmonies back and forth. Part of me has always strongly believed that if I'd ever been discovered, my singing career would've lasted close to a full five minutes, but some childhood dreams are never realized. Unfortunately, nervous laughter made the road wavy while fluffy, grey balls skittered off the asphalt, the squirrel population ignorant to the fact that wandering the road meant certain destruction.

Sliding my car in the garage was a small miracle. Plastic bag in hand, I did my best to sneak up the stairs and back to the commode.

Husband yelled from the living room. "You get the

Coke? Babe?"

I stopped. "I...I forgot. Sorry." I clutched the plastic bag and told it to stop crumpling so loudly.

"Oh. No worries, I'll get it later."

I laughed. "That's a relief, because those drug dealers kept pushing me around and saying, 'We know you're working for the cops.' And then I was all like, 'No, I'm not, yo.' And then I left and came back here, followed by minimal gunfire." *Yeah, you go get your Cherry Coke. I've gotta go whiz on a couple hundred more sticks and try not to smack my head on the bathtub when I black out from shock. When you hear the thud, please don't first assume the dog's died.*

A quick sprint upstairs, and it was just me, two hundred pregnancy tests, and a bladder full of Gatorade I'd chugged during the NASCAR race home. After passing more water than a fancy, moderately priced pitcher from Pottery Barn, I had a neat row of magic wands confirming that I was the one heading to Mordor. Someone had to carry the prego ring and it wasn't Frodo. Or a hobbit. The situation smacked of intimacy and too much Tolkien.

"Honey? You wanna go to the bookstore?" Man-Beast the Impregnator was shouting at me. News the size of a hippo's bra was getting ready to drop on the man, and he wanted to go to the bookstore. I did a quick run-through of the conversation.

"So, I'm pregnant."

"That's nice, but we really need a new table atlas and some over-priced letterhead."

"I said that I'm pregnant."

"So you're saying you don't want to shop for new letterhead?"

Clearly, now was not the time. But maybe we did need some letterhead. Bookstores always had the cutest novelty items. How many times had I imagined clutching my heaving, corseted bosom while I poured my heart and soul into a leather-bound, pressed-leaf journal? All the while leaning against a secluded oak set at the very back of Jane Austen's backyard. I'd write in a cozy place set between the stables and where they maintained my seven different carriages. And Mr. Darcy would walk up and say, "I like your journal. Barnes and Noble?"

I needed to focus.

"Sure. Just, uh, let me get ready." A palm found my forehead with an impressive, sweaty force.

The words wouldn't come out, so I got my coat and spent the entire ride staring into space like a cat with dementia. At least cats had motherly instincts. I'd held firmly to the belief that my "mother" gene had been withheld at birth. Twenty-five years of getting to know myself confirmed that hamster herding would be a safer profession than letting me rear a child. Sure, I was the oldest of ten kids, but that just meant I was great at dictating to shorter people, not birthing them. My mom had done that, and she'd had loins of steal. My loins were probably made of Styrofoam that melted at anything above room temperature.

A brisk clip from the parking lot deposited me in front of the pregnancy section. I'd shoved Husband towards an area having nothing to do with babies, like how to hunt small game with a spork during the Apocalypse. The smells of new books and uppity people drinking coffee and pretending to read Dickens calmed me as I ran my hand down the glossy spines of books with enlarged bellies printed on them. Realizing I'd stumbled on the world's largest collection of books on how to get pregnant, I mused whether they'd included the essentials: *First, one must drink two entire bottles of pinot. Now, take care to drink both bottles, otherwise, when your husband lunges at you like a giant puma, you might dodge out of the way. Full body contact is a must.*

My mother's face popped into my consciousness, mouthing something about a river and Egypt. Denial. That's what people called it. It felt kind of fuzzy and warm, but smelled like wet ferret. I was pregnant and I needed to let the Impregnator know. Looking for books was dumb. I was dumb. The baby wasn't dumb. It, at least, had made it pretty clear it was there and, I realized suddenly, would probably look like me. Poor thing. He or she would have my lack of cheek bones and forever look like a shocked squirrel in gathering season.

When we got home, Husband looked darling, like a baby deer or hand-knit socks for a pug. A pregnant vampire, I latched my eyes onto his face and soaked in the final sight of a man with no cares. My imaginary, pointy teeth sucked in the smile, easy laughter, and arm casually thrown around me. We'd made it home and burrowed down in our favorite spot on the couch. *Okay, Paige, just do it already. You're such a wiener. Not even of the Ball Park variety. Just an off-brand wiener.*

I patted a throw pillow, gently. "So." Startled by the

sound of my voice, the dog woke up, farted, and stared at me. For those of you who don't know, a dog fart is a fantastic start to breaking news of any import.

I blinked through the smell. "How would you feel about there being four of us around here instead of three?" Dead silence. I watched the information stream flow from the ears, to the eyes, down to the nether-regions, and back again.

"You're pregnant?"

I nodded. "Uh huh."

Somewhere on the front porch, a group of crickets the size of the Vienna Boy's Choir began Handel's "Messiah." But, after a minute that lasted for an hour, something happened. From under the shaggy brown hair, blue eyes started relaxing, brows un-knit themselves, and a sweet smile spread like butter over a hot bagel, reminding me how much I loved bagels—or waffles, if whoever was serving breakfast was out of bagels. In that moment, though, reality was bacon. Because, as we all know, bacon trumps all, metaphorically and actually.

"That's great," he said, planting a kiss on my lips.

Tension left my butt crack. I smiled back. "So you're happy? I mean, I am too, just in shock. You would not believe how many tests I took." As I attempted to execute some sort of international sign for pregnancy test, my hands flapped around like a seal in distress.

"More than one?"

I snorted. "Everyone else in the city's going to have to guess whether they're pregnant. Oh, that reminds me, if you see a charge for five hundred dollars' worth of pregnancy tests, just go back to your regularly scheduled day. We did it."

But the Impregnator wasn't looking at me anymore.

Two months prior to this meeting of the minds, I'd been watching *Shark Week* on Discovery Channel, paying special attention when they did the shark attack reenactments. Something about the pure terror splashed across the shark victims' faces always riveted and horrified me, and made me clench my family-sized bag of Oreos in terror. That particular brand of shock had found its way onto my floral-print sofa and made a home on Husband's face. A baby shark had swum upstream and bitten Husband and me in our collective rear. One thing was certain; we were definitely going to need a bigger boat. And more Oreos.

2
Ding Dongs

The sheet was thin and offered my lady parts about as much coverage as an old dish towel. An arctic wind made its way around my ankles, slapped my nether regions, and rushed back out again. I couldn't help wondering how all those starlets ran around exposing their goods in public; it was cold and frightening. Beggars couldn't be choosers, though. I needed these people to help me figure out how to get my child from uterus to Earth in three, easy steps. Like making brownies. But I wasn't even that good at making brownies. Hopefully I'd be able to meet with some sort of specialized task force who could bake and birth babies.

Nurse Ratched opened the door. She wasn't nearly as terrifying as the fictional one, but I don't take kindly to strangers who order me to strip and wait by myself in a refrigerator. All things considered, it had to be an interesting work experience. Conversations around the dinner table were probably interesting. "Yeah, I left at least ten women naked and terrified in rooms created to simulate the Arctic. This meatloaf is to die for, though. I used whole croutons instead of bread crumbs. It'll be a winner at the cook-off on Saturday. What? No, it's not inhumane, honey. We give them a motel pillowcase to throw over their girls."

"The doctor will see you now." She gave me a quick smile and opened the door. Behind her, a man old enough to be my father walked in. Thankfully, not my actual father. I'd been married for a month, but had a distinct feeling he'd still want an explanation.

He smiled. "Well, first of all, congratulations."

"Thanks." I closed my legs a little tighter and rolled into a protective ball like I'd seen hedgehogs do on the Discovery Channel. Why couldn't I have been born with quills to cover my restricted areas? Hedgehogs were so lucky. If I rolled out the door, would they notice?

"So, I understand you took a couple tests. All positive?"

"Uh, yeah. That means I'm pregnant. At least, I'm pretty sure. I remember seeing something on TV that explained how you can tell if you are. Not sure I believe everything about the storks and dowsing rods though. If you guys want to give me another test, that's fine." My eyes leveled with his nametag. "Like I always say, a test isn't conclusive until one takes it five hundred and one times. Let's do it."

The doctor's bushy eyebrows rose slightly, but he went on. "No, not necessary. Those tests are pretty accurate. If you got more than one positive, it's pretty certain."

"Are you sure? Because I'm pretty sure I saw that little gem stitched on a throw pillow somewhere."

"Now then, I want you to do several things from here on out." He began listing off my pregnancy assignments while I used my hand to catch the ignorant drool pooling from the corner of my mouth: lots of water, plenty of sleep, no smoking, eat as healthy as possible, lay off crack, avoid landmines, etc. "And if you feel any persistent, sharp pains, contact the office right away."

Check, check...wait. Pain? I tightened my sheet. "What do you mean, pain? Like if I need a Band-Aid for a blister? Or the kind where Michael Myers finally finds you in the *Halloween* movies and you're stabbed more than a turkey on Thanksgiving? And you're yelling, but no one hears you because you're not a virgin and you decided to go see what the noise was in the barn, even though you were distinctly told to stay with the group? And then you know you're not going to be in the sequel because there's no way you'll survive being attacked with a pitchfork? That type of pain?"

He assured me it was somewhere in the middle, that I was a smart person and would know it if I felt it, and to do my best not to call 911 or run screaming down the street in my underwear. I needed to come in to the office instead.

With that, he exited and left me and my friend, the sheet, to ponder the word "pain" and what it meant in the context of pregnancy.

Turns out, we wouldn't have to ponder for long.

I'd always considered myself in the ninety-nine percent of the population who loves sleep. Everyone knows the remaining one percent is vampires and insomniacs watching re-runs of *Cheers*. But, for the third night in a row, I'd been yanked from the magical beach on which I spent most of my dreamtime. Annoyed, I watched as golden sands and my beach pals, Justin Timberlake and Josh Hartnett, turned and waved goodbye. "Hey!" I shouted. "We're supposed to build sandcastles and talk about how you wish more Hollywood actresses had my naturally wavy hair and intellectual pep. Really, no one's up for a game of Trivial Pursuit?" But I couldn't wave back because, when I came to, an invisible stick was poking me so hard in the abdomen that my eyeballs convinced themselves there was two of everything in the room. That included our TV, and I knew we were too poor for that to be true.

By the time the sun showed its face, I'd spent the majority of the dark hours writhing like a grizzly who'd eaten a Toyota. This was serious. Dr. Bushy Brows echoed in my head, "Persistent, sharp pains are bad." Bad. Exactly. This was bad. Not pitchfork through my temple bad, but not good.

Ignoring my intestines as they liquefied and fought to dribble out of my body, I rolled to my side. "Honey, I think I'm dying. Actually, I'm sure of it. Thoughts?"

He rolled over and stared at me. "Dying? It happened again? Are you alright?"

I coughed. "Um, if my abdomen reenacting the storming of the beaches at Normandy eighty times in the last five hours is normal, then yeah, I'm alright. What's sad is that we're still so young, and I haven't done anything on our bucket list, like teach you how to make the bed how I like it."

Pooling our knowledge of *Rosemary's Baby* and *The*

Omen, we came to a group decision that what was happening probably wasn't normal and required someone with medical knowledge, or possibly a giant bottle of holy water. I called the doctor.

The nurse sounded concerned. "Mrs. Kellerman, that sounds like something the doctor would like to check on. You say it's been happening for three days? You better come right in. Wait, who's Rosemary, and what about her baby?"

She was right, it probably wasn't a demon baby, but that didn't stop my brain from running amuck in the fields of "what if?" land. What if I was losing the baby? What if I was hemorrhaging internally and both of us weren't going to make it? I hadn't made a will yet, seen the Great Wall of China, or made it as a contestant on Jeopardy. I'd never be able to stroke Alex Trebek's mustache like a small baby lemur.

Husband and I made the short drive to the doctor's office, checked in, and spent thirty minutes contemplating our future while we waited to be called. Waiting in the doctor's office is nothing short of nerve-wracking when you're sure bad news awaits you. No amount of outdated *People* magazines can distract you. Not even the ones with the coupons that haven't expired yet, but you don't want to take them because you're not sure if that counts as stealing or not. But, man, you could really use a dollar off Glade air fresheners. You love the scent of vanilla.

"Kellerman?"

The pain in my abdomen subsided just enough for me to hear my name, jump up, and sprint at the lady with the clipboard, like a mountain lion at a hiker. "Me. That's me," I said, half waving, half pointing at her face. "You meant the lady dying out here while everyone else watches, right? Because, as luck would have it, I just happen to be that woman. Nice to meet you."

The nurse managed a brisk smile that made it clear she'd seen my particular brand of desperation before, and motioned for us to follow her through the maze of doors and sanitary stations, finally depositing us in a little white room. "Wait here. The doctor will see you shortly."

As soon as the door closed, the familiar feeling of my butt crack tensing popped up. "Shortly? I could be dead by then. Have these people no sense of urgency?"

Three seconds later, Dr. Bushy Brows strolled in.

"Hello, Mrs. Kellerman. I understand you've been having some pain." He looked at me like I wasn't dying. The nerve. How dare he think I wasn't dying? I assumed he'd been to medical school. Could identify if someone was about to pass on. Surely he recognized this in me, but was, perhaps, playing coy until he knew what type of insurance I carried.

I nodded. "Yes, very persistent, for the last three days. You said not to panic. So here I am, not panicking. Ironically, me not panicking looks amazingly similar to when I am panicking, leading most people to just be done with it and label me neurotic."

We exchanged glances. Just enough interaction to assure me the man thought my unborn baby's mother was raised in a station wagon in Appalachia.

"I see. Well, let's check the heartbeat."

Like a land-mired orca, I flopped down on the wax

paper and let him run the small Doppler across my stomach and abdomen. His lips pursed as though all his thinking went on in his mouth. "I can't hear anything. We'd better do a sonogram."

My heart was gone—pure shock caused it to drop out my butt and onto the floor. I couldn't speak, and just nodded as Husband and I were directed to the room with the sonogram machine.

Two zombies, we followed the nurse to another white room where we were greeted by Nurse Perky Pants. Unfortunately, no one had informed her that our parenting dreams were currently being crushed and it would be better for her to just hand me some coffee and not make direct eye contact. If she had, I wouldn't have wanted to tar, feather, and leave her to dry in the sun when she greeted us with, "Hi! How're you guys today? Why don't you hop on the table and we'll take a look? This your first sonogram?"

"Uh huh." I said, as I hoisted my dejected form onto the grey foam table. Normally, things that are comically spongy make my day. They practically beg, "Lay down. Roll around. Try to leave your head print. But don't laugh. You still want to be seen as an adult." The grey foam was ill-timed.

The nurse finished readying the machine and sat poised to tell me my future. "Make yourself comfortable, relax, and we'll take a look."

"Oh, and while you're in there, do me a favor and change the oil, will ya? I've got a fifty-percent-off coupon I've just been dying to use."

"What was that?"

"Nothing."

I reclined and tried to remain calm, which would've been easier if she hadn't been waving something at me. "Ok, now I'll just insert this." She lurched towards me, brandishing what looked like a sick magician's prop. "You're not that far along, so it'll have to be done internally."

I wanted to ask her if Dumbledore knew she'd stolen Harry's wand, but I held it back.

Instead, I bit my lip, embraced the inevitable, and let the lady do her business.

While Sally Sunshine poked around, I took deep breaths, concentrating on the ceiling, the glowing monitor, how on earth Italy came to be shaped like a boot—anything except what was going on down south.

"Now, let's see...Oh...Ah."

I sat up a little. "Did you find the library card I lost last year? I've got books on hold."

But Husband had already seen. Our eyes met, and traveled to the glowing box harboring our future.

Now, neither of us is a doctor. In fact, science has always been my worst subject. On the ACTs, I'd been so perplexed by the mating of squirrels and subsequent theories of squirrel duplication that I'd almost broken into hysterics, impaled myself on my neatly sharpened No. 2 pencil, and died the gory death only multiple choice can bring. But, by gum, my saintly mother had taught me how to add. Deep down, my brain cells knew one plus one is two. I'd sworn it would never be good for anything except figuring out how much change I needed to dig out of my couch cushions to buy cigarettes, but, at that moment, simple math helped me realize what I was looking at.

Two glowing orbs seemed to radiate the light of sudden shock. Uteruses only divide in half for a couple reasons I know of; you're either some type of mythological creature that turns to stone when she looks in a mirror, or you're having twins. Sweet nectar of the gods, we were having twins.

For the second time, our eyes met, and Husband and I stared at each other like poached codfish.

"Well, congratulations. Looks like you're having twins." Perky Pants couldn't contain her excitement.

"Twins? As in two of them? Like how you always get two Ding Dongs to a package, even though you only thought you needed one, but you end up eating both because you can't control yourself?"

"Uh huh."

"Oh."

I couldn't contain my bladder. I raised my hand. "Ahherrohhmmphh." It wasn't English, but, somehow, the situation didn't call for English. It called for slipping my sweatpants back on, walking out of the room, running into a couple of nurses, smacking into a wall, and asking the receptionist if she could "Wake me up now, because I'll be late for work and have no sick days, even though it's only October, but I had to use that last one because there was a marathon of *Angel* on."

On the ride home, Husband stared ahead. "So, um,

what now?"

I kicked my feet up on the dash and tried to see the last bits of my youth through the rain-slicked windshield. "The wipers work really well in here. We should drive your car more often. What kind of wipers are these? Low squeak factor, high resolution? One time, in college, my windshield wiper went crazy and tried to stab me through the glass. I had to tie it down with a pink bandana until I got back to campus. True story."

Looking dazed, Husband stared forward, hands on the wheel, one eyebrow raised. "Not really what I meant."

"We haven't told anyone yet. I'd like to tell my mom first, if you don't mind." Our little car felt more claustrophobic than a cone-shaped bra. If I didn't tell her first, someone else would, and that someone else wouldn't hear about it for the next thirty Christmases in a row. Besides, the woman had a pack of children; if anyone knew whether we needed to invest in two cribs or two straight jackets, it was her. If we told her real nice, maybe she'd let us share that padded cell she'd put herself on the waiting list for. Maybe, by now, she'd decided to simply become a hermit and rent a nice place in Bora Bora, where we'd never think to look.

Husband pulled off the highway and headed toward my parents' house. A few turns, an unsuccessful attempt at slicking down my eyebrows to look presentable, and we cruised into the driveway.

If he was nervous, he didn't show it. For his sake, I'd calculated the months a zillion times on the trip over. We were married in July, pregnant in September, which meant I'd gotten pregnant a month after the wedding.

There wouldn't be any haggling over whether these kids had been conceived in the back of a truck, right before I'd speed-walked to Handel down the aisle.

"Ready?" Husband squeezed my hand.

"I'd say I was born ready, but the woman would know that or not. Let's go get some advice from the Dalai Lama of Deliveries."

My youngest sister opened the door. We stepped into the entryway and followed her to the dining room, where my mom sat at the table.

"Wise one."

"Hi, guys. Come on in. You two okay?" Her eyes worked us over. "You look like something the cat dragged in."

"Cats."

"What?"

"Nothing. Just stopped by to say hi," I said.

She set her coffee down, rested her chin on her palm, and raised an eyebrow. For a lady who'd manufactured an entire soccer team, cleaned more than a freelance maid, and yelled more than Al Pacino in *Dog Day Afternoon*, she was really quite pretty. Her chestnut hair was still winning in the race against grey, and her face wasn't nearly as lined as you'd expect from a person who'd once threatened to "sell all of you to gypsies and move to China."

She looked us over. "What is it?"

Shuffling forward, I set the sonogram pictures down in front of her and stepped back. She smiled as she began to flip through the mostly black photos, stopping on the lone picture depicting the two glowing orbs. Her smile grew. "Well, how about that?"

"We came here for an accurate estimate. How many years do we have before they rise up and kill us?"

"Guys, this is great news. Congratulations!"

Husband smiled. "Thanks." I felt sure he was growing more comfortable with the idea of admitting he was the father.

"So, you two excited?" She was laughing. The woman was actually laughing.

"Yep, excited." I rubbed my face with my sweaty shirt sleeve. "But let's talk turkey."

"Yes?"

"Well, turkey and some mustard. I'll probably need a sandwich. But, besides that, what are we going to need here? Two of everything, or just a straight jacket to share? I know you know. So don't hold out."

"Sweetheart, you'll be fine."

Unconvinced, I paced back and forth while filling her in on the events that had led us to the doctor's office in the first place. After a while, we decided to head out. Mom hugged me and held the door open. "You guys let me know if you need anything."

I locked eyes with her. "And you let me know when your cell has an opening."

"What?"

"Nothing. Just think about it." And with that, all four of us walked back to the car.

3
Morning Sickness

For the third morning in a row, I'd slunk into the bathroom and, clad only in underwear and a frown, mounted the slim, grey scale. The familiar "hung over but not hung over" feeling crept over me while I watched the numbers tick by. The scale didn't lie. I'd lost five pounds. That was almost as much as one of those mid-size pumpkins Martha Stewart was always trying to get me to turn into toilet paper holders or homing beacons for senior citizens.

If there's anything I know about weight, it's that it makes a huge difference when buying bananas in bulk. Unfortunately, I hadn't really put much thought into the subject before I got pregnant. Therefore, I was curious when I observed the five-pound difference in my own weight. I stood on one foot and looked again, but the digital numbers stayed the same. The morning sickness experience was throwing me for a loop, and I'd never been a fan of loops. Except in bows. Bows needed loops. Cul-de-sacs also needed loops. I'd lived on one growing up. It hadn't been so bad.

As I pulled out an outfit for work, I lamented to Husband, who was lying face down on his pillow.

"I lost five pounds."

"That's great, babe. You're gonna look like a rock star." Which came out just muffled enough to sound like "You look like a boxcar."

"That's the problem. I should look like a boxcar, a big, fat boxcar, but I just haven't been hungry. It's more like I want to stab food until it dies. Then curl in a ball. Then write morose letters of farewell to nachos. Cheese, twas like I hardly knew ye."

Husband rolled over and squinted at me. "You saw a boxcar? You can't be pregnant and wandering around train tracks."

Ignoring him, I spelunked into some spandex leggings and tugged on a shirt. "Here I am, supposed to be gaining weight, and instead it turns out I may have to email Kate Moss to borrow a pair of pants."

Dear Ms. Moss,

How are things? You have a lot more money than I do, so I'll assume things are, at least, "OK." I hope you're well and no one's photographed you in a compromising situation, as of late. If you'd be so kind, please Fed-Ex me some spare chinos. As it turns out, nothing tastes good and I've lost a few pounds. By the way, drugs are bad. If you want to know how to stay skinny, just get pregnant. It's a lot more fun than dipping cotton balls in orange juice.

Sincerely,

Paige Kellerman

P.S—I've noticed you execute an extremely effortless "smoky eye" and "rouged, yet gaunt cheek bone." Feel free to return pointers with your response.

The past few weeks had been rough. Nothing looked appetizing. Food and I had always had a great relationship. I was the girl everyone talked about behind her back. The hussy who'd taken a cheeseburger to bed with her the night of her twenty-first birthday, and had waved it shamelessly and bun-less at her best friend's mother the next morning. Once, a few people from my church found out I'd not only romanced a bowl of guacamole on a Friday night, but had also cuddled with it until sunrise. Needless to say, the quilting group was down a member.

A couple girls at work gave me some pregnancy books so I could follow the miracles inside me. The *What To Expect When You're Expecting* lady told me I might be sick for the first six weeks. She hadn't mentioned that I'd begin hurling burritos back at Chipotle cashiers like a poop-laden orangutan. Or that, two days prior, the sight of fried chicken would so alarm me, I'd hide under the table until Husband ate it. Our receipt had said, "Thanks for Dining at The Saucy Buffalo: Where drinks are served with the food. Your server was Gary, and he reminds you to dislodge your pregnant wife from under the bench and have a nice day."

So, after I listened to Husband accuse me of being a boxcar child, the anxiety that I was starving our unborn children began to take over. My spandex and I headed downstairs and prepared for another day of starvation. No need to pack a lunch; I had my fist to chew on while I rocked back and forth in my cubicle and wrote to Kate Moss. I wondered if company letterhead would make her take me more seriously.

All day I watched co-workers eat stacks of cookies and consume eighty-pound bags of Corn Nuts using fax cover sheets rolled into funnels, directing avalanches of ranch-flavored goodness down their gullets. By noon, I'd stolen the steak tartar a guy in accounting had brought in, and taken his kneecaps out with it. Someone had tried to cook tuna in the microwave, again. By two o'clock, I'd plotted her death and purchased maternity camo on Amazon so she wouldn't see me follow her to her car. Tuna Woman had no rights.

Thirty minutes before my shift ended, my boss walked by. "Feelin' okay?"

"I'm dying."

She smiled. "Well, that's good. Have a great weekend and don't forget to clock out."

I really hoped she was the one who'd nuked the tuna. "I will. Oh, and there's the smallest chance I'll have starved by Monday, so you'll want to spend your Saturday typing something up on Career Builder. Don't mention it's because I died, though. People don't tend to jump on those opportunities."

"What was that?"

"Umm, I have to go to the bathroom."

She smiled. "I hear pregnant ladies do that a lot."

I sighed. "We do, but it's only because we love the smooth, smooth feel of porcelain on our rear ends. It's a calming sensation. Keeps us from charging strangers."

While I drove home, I fantasized about dinner. It'd been eight hours since I'd eaten anything, and after I caught myself trying to lick the steering wheel, I knew I was in trouble. My appetite seemed to be returning. Hunger was knocking and demanded an answer. Would I be naughty and have Lucky Charms on toast? Or, perhaps, push the boundaries of decency and force the dill pickles to walk the graham cracker plank into the jar of marshmallow fluff? Stopping at a red light, I threw my head back and let out a laugh evil pirates would've been jealous of. Peanut butter on pizza. English muffins cavorting with jalapenos. It would be madness, shear madness.

By the time my car found the garage, I'd cooked up a thousand ways to make Anthony Bourdain quit his job and renounce food as a passion. Husband was sitting on the couch when I threw the door open. "Feed me."

"I will. Wanna go out to dinner tonight? Japanese steakhouse?" He dangled the last word like a carrot.

I quit gnawing the paint off the doorway just long enough to consider. "They'll feed me?"

"They'll feed you. Some friends called and they want to go out. I figured this would be a great time to break the news."

"What news?"

"The babies."

"Oh, right." I picked a chip of paint from between my front teeth. "When we paint the kitchen, I'd really like to go for a nice mocha. This off-white tastes terrible."

Husband was already off the couch. "Ok, we'll leave in five minutes."

But I didn't need five minutes to slick down my eyebrows and make myself comfortable in the passenger seat. When he finally made it to the car, my stomach was threatening to turn itself inside out, exit my body, and march back up to the kitchen. "Get in, turn the key, and drive. Drive me to food. You don't get to impregnate and then starve me. I won't stand for it."

He rolled his eyes. "Easy, it's only been two minutes."

Grabbing his belt buckle, I yanked him inside the car, positioned his hand on the key, and used it to turn the ignition. "Food. Go." Explaining that sitting next to a hungry pregnant woman was the closest thing to swimming with piranha seemed like a waste of time. If I ended up taking a chunk out of his leg because he didn't get me to the restaurant fast enough, well, he'd just have to learn the hard way.

What was usually a fifteen-minute drive to downtown turned into my stomach's equivalent of Hannibal marching elephants across the Alps. Slow and steady. Why did he have to keep stopping at stoplights? Letting old people cross at intersections? Safety didn't matter; I'd eaten my seatbelt before we'd even hit the highway, and I was halfway through the owner's manual when we pulled up to the restaurant. Chapter two had been delicious, and I'd also learned that I needed to ease the jack under the front wheel, slowly, if I wanted to get anywhere and not uselessly break an expensive piece of equipment.

"Let me out here. I'll just make my way to the kitchen." I struggled as Husband grabbed my waistband, insistent on the fact that we needed to park somewhere first. Grudgingly, I let him find a space in the parking garage and lead the way down the sidewalk and up to the steakhouse.

"Good evening." Smiling, the greeter ushered us into the lush bar.

I bowed low. "Good evening to you, sir. Is the food ready?"

Behind me, Husband coughed. "Babe, we have to wait for everyone else to get here."

"Muffin cake, everyone else isn't knocking on Death's door." Letting go of the greeter's apron, I padded to the gleaming bar, hopped up on a stool, and looked around.

"Ma'am, can I get you anything?" As he dried a glass, the bartender looked me over.

"Yes. I'd like a new husband, shaken, not stirred." My thumb hitched sideways. "This one doesn't feed me."

"He doesn't?"

"Nope. I'm having his baby, and he won't even get me an English muffin. How's that for gratitude?"

Without a word, the bartender slid me a glass of water and a plastic bowl of peanuts. "The Circle of Life" playing in the back of my head, I hoisted the bowl above my head and displayed my prey. A prehistoric growl escaped me as I tipped the germ-infested bowl, ever so slightly, preparing to enjoy a dinner made entirely of bar fodder.

"Oh...no....Honey, put those down." Husband had my wrist in his left hand and was wrestling the bowl away from me with his right. "Don't worry. Look, Mike's here." The rest of our group had arrived and was heading towards the bar, waving.

My lip trembled. "But...p-p-peanuts." Too late. I'd already been enveloped in a thick crowd of "hellos," each one pulling me further from the plastic bowl. I began pacing back and forth like a sheep dog, making circles around the group of five, hoping against hope that I could somehow convince them to sit down.

My eighth pass was interrupted by one of our single friends. "Doin' alright there?"

I quit jogging in place long enough to answer. "Great. You?"

"Good. Umm...can I get you something to drink? Beer? Some sheep to herd?"

I waved him off. "No, thanks. Do you know if they actually serve food here?"

Before he could answer, a man in a red vest beckoned us to follow him through the dining room. Tables full of happy people enjoying chicken, rice, and delicious-smelling soups flanked me on both sides. Overwhelmed, I stopped and tapped an eighty-year-old woman on the shoulder. "Are you going to finish that steak? To be fair, I think I may need it more than you. Think about it. Will one steak kebab really postpone the inevitable? Probably not enough to eat that whole thing." My hand was suddenly in Husband's and I was being dragged towards the back of the restaurant.

I took a seat around the "table," which was actually a huge grill with seats close enough to singe my eyebrows, possibly evening them out. I mentally referenced my copy of *What To Expect*, my right brain flipping through the index: *toes, tinkle, trauma, trying to fit in the shower*. Nothing on torture. How could that be? Surely the author had tips for starving mothers forced to watch chefs make flaming onion volcanoes which belched mockery and disdain. Disdain is the worst. Smells like a bologna-loving helper monkey left out in the rain with no coat.

In his little, white hat, our chef was hurriedly greasing down the grill and organizing ingredients. Like a flash, he'd sliced an onion, filled it with something flammable, and lit it on fire. While everyone "oohed" and "aahed", I kicked at my chair impatiently and raised my hand. "Sir, I know you're really busy creating a fabulous vegetable circus, but could I get a raw pepper to chew on? Or were you planning on making tiny pepper elephants to throw in that volcano?"

Rubbing my back, like a prize-fighter's coach, Husband tried to soothe me. "Hang in there, babe. It'll be ready in a minute. Who's my girl?"

"I dunno, but she better get here before I chew a hole through your coat. I hope she doesn't mind watching pepper elephant massacres, either. It's about to get real in here. Real and refreshing. Find me some dressing."

The intoxicating smells had nearly driven me to the brink of insanity when the stocky, sweat-drenched chef smacked his spatula against the grill, making me jump. Quickly, he began throwing food on plates and serving it around the table. Under my breath, I whispered, "Me, me, me, please pick me." And, just as the delicate china plate was launched my way, it happened; my dreams crumbled, my body recoiled from the grill. I suddenly needed what was on that smoking-hot slab of metal as much as a vampire wanted a soul.

"Ok, sweetheart, I know you've been really patient, so here ya go." Husband presented the white plate like it was a brand new chicken-free Lexus, setting it down gently in front of the pregnant beast.

"I can't."

He looked confused. "You can't what?"

"Eat."

"Seriously?"

"Do zombies hate hand to hand combat?"

"So that's a yes?"

I considered. "No, I just really wanted an unbiased opinion. The last zombie I asked wasn't very forthcoming. Of course that's a yes. My morning sickness is back. And she's angry."

By the time everyone had finished eating, I'd used my tears to ply my napkin into a swan, a deer, and a rabbit re-enacting the Battle of the Bulge. When the last fork-full of rice signaled I would indeed die and be entombed in the cool, savory, steakhouse catacombs, Husband decided to share our big news.

Grinning like only an Impregnator can, he passed around the pictures while squeezing my hand. Whether to keep me from fainting or to make it clear that it was my uterus everyone was looking at, I'll never know.

After all the excitement and congratulatory remarks had been made, a figure blurred by hunger looked at me and said, "Well, you look great. How you feelin'?"

"Full of joy. It's the only thing I'm running on."

He laughed. "What do you want to do after dinner?"

"Write."

"Write?"

"Right. Me and Kate Moss have a lot to talk about. But I have to visit the train tracks, first."

Husband smoothed my hair, gave me some tooth-picks to chew on, and dragged me out the door.

4
Zombies and Harlots

When a woman's pregnant, nothing makes itself more apparent to her than the un-tapped market. As I gazed at the rows of corsets, wigs, and stockings, I couldn't help noticing the lack of attractive costumes for expectant mothers. There was a section fully stocked with everything one would need to parade down the street dressed as Moby Dick, the blurb on the plastic practically selling itself. "Are you looking to repel every man at the costume party? Complete with working spout!" But a Flirty Nurse or Dominatrix Debbie was out of the question.

Husband came up behind me and pointed to the picture of a saucy-looking bimbo in a "police uniform."

"How about that one? She looks comfortable."

"I'm pregnant." Looking around the corner, I searched for a set of plastic handcuffs I could use to secure him to the rack of plastic axes and leave him there. "When was the last time you saw a pregnant police woman bust a crack house? I simply can't count the times I've seen one break down a door and yell, 'Drop the pipe or I'll eat all your Oreos.'"

He shrugged. "Suit yourself, but there has to be something here you want to dress up in." He wiggled a plastic bag showing a picture of a skinny blond with a fire hose.

Before my misguided soul mate could hold up another hermetically sealed package containing a corset and no self-esteem, I turned my bloated self around and marched towards the makeup section. It was the day before Halloween, and the costume shop was bustling with kids whose parents had just remembered it was their job to supply a Batman cape, teenage kids searching for a mask that would hide their identity as they left flaming poop on Mrs. Dinkmeyer's doorstep, and, of course, herds of skinny twenty-somethings looking for the perfect harlot costume for the evening.

A few feet away, a waif of a brunette slipped on a red wig and laughed at her friend, a petite blond trying to figure out if the fishnets or the five-inch spiked heels would make her look more like Amelia Earhart. They must've settled on going naked because after a few minutes of deliberation, they left the goods where they were and me standing by myself.

Having gotten over my feud with every food known to man, the morning sickness had cleared, my belly had started protruding, and I was now the proud owner of a miniature shelf like a backwoods gas station attendant's beer belly. I'd found myself having to resist the urge to shout, "Fill 'er up? I can do that. Carwash? Value pack of cigarette lighters? I got this stuffed Garfield that'd look great in your back winda'." Another quick search of the

pregnancy manuals had confirmed there wasn't a section on "extreme muffin-top syndrome," only pictures of
twiggy women with bumps as adorable as baby bunnies
stuck to the front of them. I was neither a bunny, nor cute.

Belly resting on knees, I squatted and looked through
the stacks of makeup and fake teeth. Maybe there was a
three-step DIY bunny kit waiting to be snatched up. If I
asked nicely, maybe Husband would ball up some toilet
paper and Scotch tape it to my rear. I'd make the costume
party a hit. "Who, me?" I'd fan my chest. "No, not a Play-
boy bunny, just your garden variety stewing rabbit. If you
get me lemonade, I'll give you my tail so you can TP the
neighbor's RV."

Hoisting myself up on a nearby rack of werewolf den-
tures, I'd all but given up the idea of celebrating Halloween when something caught my eye, and it was beautiful—shards of glass and all. The tagline made me want to
shoplift it then and there: "Want to make your loved ones
think you've been in a horrifying car accident?"

Yes.

"Have you ever wanted to look like the walking
dead?"

Yes.

"Pregnant and no one's looking your way this Halloween?"

Affirmative.

I hadn't felt such an overwhelming love since the time
I forgot my wedding vows but gave Husband a nod and
a handshake that meant, "I do." Holding the plastic package firmly against my chest, I skipped back around the

gravestones, hanging skeletons, and his and hers Twinkie costumes, until I came upon my other half. "I found it."

He gave me a wink. "Must be the smallest French maid uniform known to man."

"I'm going to be a zombie." I shuffled the first steps to "Thriller."

His face fell as I turned the package around. "A zombie? And apparently one that was in a hideous car accident. At least you'll be coming home with me. You sure you don't want a sexy costume?"

But I was already swiping my Visa and then headed to the car. Every Halloween before, I'd dressed as something sultry. This year I'd actually celebrate the holiday and do it the way it was supposed to be done, by becoming as craptastically ugly as I could muster. The world would have to wait another year for my "Amorous Anne Boleyn." This year I was going to be the Undead Glass-Faced Prego from everyone's nightmares, shambling about and moaning, "Piiiiie. Piiiiie. Boston Cream Piiiie. Excuse me, sir, after I eat your brain, I'd like some piiiiie."

The sun couldn't go down fast enough. By the last light of day, I began crafting my masterpiece. Hair in a ponytail, shelf-belly covered by surgical scrubs I'd bought from Goodwill so I could be a "nurse" at my office's half-assed celebration of a Halloween party, I grabbed a glob of white paint and spread it around with a sponge, careful to cover the bases of the "glass shards," which turned out to be some sort of rubber from the deepest jungles of Glasstonia. Cheeks, neck, collarbone—a few seconds transformed me into a pregnant woman George A. Romero could take home to his mother.

Shambling to the bedroom where Husband was napping, presumably to gain the strength to have me drive him around all night, I padded through the doorway and over to the lump under the quilt. "Well, hello there. See anything you like?" I poked the blanket. "Time to get ready to take me out on the town."

Two eyes reluctantly slid open. "Wow. You look…"

"Like the woman you fell in love with? Yes, I know. Now let's get you ready. This much sexy can't go out without a date."

"Maybe it can. Has it given it the old college try yet?"

"To the make-up chair." My white hands dragged him to the bathroom, and with steady hand, applied the werewolf kit he'd picked out.

"I think you got your fake blood on my snout."

"I think you got your snout in my fake blood. By the way, there's no such thing as a Jamaican werewolf." With that, I helped him slip on his Hawaiian-print shirt, grabbed the keys, and the Zombie and the Wolf Mon stepped out.

***

Two parties later, my pregnant feet couldn't take any more. Unfortunately, werewolves have an irritating ability to drink for hours on end. As I inched Husband closer to the door, I couldn't help speculating that an impregnated Mrs. Van Helsing would've already scratched her stretch marks and put a silver bullet in this particular specimen. He nuzzled his snout in my shoulder.

"Just one more party. A few of the guys are headed to a little get-together and want us to come. We'll only stay for a little bit and then head home. I promise."

I shook my bottle of sparkling grape juice at him. "This pretend wine can only carry me so far."

"Can you pretend for a little longer?"

"That I like you?"

"Exactly."

"No."

The night had been fairly fun. True, I'd been the only pregnant zombie at both parties, but there'd also been a welcome absence of busty, corseted costumes. Now, my internal clock was telling me it was time to go home, melt a batch of candy bars, apply a Snickers facial, and eat myself to sleep. But I wasn't in an entirely horrid mood, so I said it. "Ok, we'll stop by for a bit, but then we're headed home."

Ten minutes later, Husband had come closer to extinction than an albino panda with five legs.

"I'm going to leave you. So help me, I'll eat your brains and take the house."

He patted my thigh. "Try to relax. I'm going to grab a drink and we'll stay for five minutes."

"You do realize you should never tell a pregnant woman to 'relax' at a drunken party in full swing, correct? Never tell her to 'relax,' period. She doesn't know what it means, and assumes the person addressing her is speaking a lost dialect of Swahili."

Actually, studies have shown that three out of four people who tell a woman to relax end up dead. Like a gazelle invited to a lion's family reunion or a college student who stumbles into Nordstrom, the impregnated woman will always feel out of place where everyone's inebriated and dressed like Twelfth Avenue hookers.

What'd been sold to me as a "little get-together" was actually an all-inclusive gala sponsored by the local chapter of the Ladies of the Night and the Friends of the Clothes-less. Clinging to the un-painted doorway, I watched half-naked Mary Todd Lincolns dance on coffee tables, questionable Jackie Os swing from light fixtures, and Amelia Earhart saunter to the keg in her fishnets, blink until someone filled her pilot cap with Coors, and bend over so everyone could see her Bermuda Triangle. I'd tried as hard as I could to avoid them, but the harlots had still found me.

"Oooh, you look so gross."

The sound of her voice made me turn.

A bunny without pants shoved her finger in my face and poked at the glass shard sitting above my eye. "It just looks so real."

"Hold on."

She cocked her head. "What are you doing?"

"Checking my pocket copy of *The Big Book of Pregnancy Etiquette*, I flipped through the pages. "Ahh, just as I suspected, I'm not allowed to slap a ho, even if she's just pretending for Halloween. Look, it says so right here in the index." My pointer finger tapped the page. "Right there next to 'Carrot juice helps with second trimester gas'."

Her boyfriend guided her away just as Husband returned, and before I could rip her tail off and stuff it in her ear. "How we doing?"

"Great. Wishing I could join in." I gestured to a girl using a Band-Aid as a skirt, who was shouting, "Who wants to play Twister?" while standing on her head.

Husband suddenly looked as frightened as he should've been the whole time. "You ready to go?"

I shook my head. "No, we can't leave now. I heard the group discussion on Thoreau's effect on Transcendentalism starts at midnight. It's my turn to bring the cookies. If I don't show, they'll never invite me back."

That night, as I lay under my Butterfinger facial, I swore vengeance on the Halloween harlots. Maybe the market for maternity costumes was sparse, but it didn't matter. Next year I would get my abs back, dress as a ninja, and challenge every single one of them to a duel. And, if that failed, dressing as a cop and raiding crack houses didn't sound that bad either.

5
Alcohol is Only Overrated if You Hate Fun

"You're not missing out on anything." Husband took a long, sensuous swig on his beer bottle and smiled at me, his body visibly relaxing as Coor's Light distributed equal parts alcohol and sedation through his entire personage. I sat there watching him, trying not to fly across the room like a whale with rabies and slap him silly with one of my swollen fins.

"I'm not?"

"Nah. Beer's pretty overrated." He sank down in the sofa. "I mean, it's not even that good."

"You seem to enjoy it."

He waved me away. "A mild exaggeration. It's just there and it's cold, so I drink it. I wouldn't say I enjoy it."

I motioned to the table. "It must have been torture to get through those other five then. That last one looked particularly cold and refreshing."

"Yeah, that last one was a doozy. Before I drank it, I had every care in the world. Now? Nothing. It's excruciating, really."

I stopped working on my "Top One Hundred Things I Worry About, At All Points In the Day" list I'd been scratching onto the coffee table. "Sounds hard. I worried all day. About the babies. About finances. About how I put on a pair of underwear last week and still can't find it. Although, I suspect fat fold number three, the one just below my love handles. I'm thinking about making fly-ers, if you wanna help me find some telephone poles lat-er. Strangely enough, having a beer sounds like it would make all of those things a little easier."

Husband closed his eyes and breathed a relaxed sigh. "Nah. Sounds like you have all that stuff under control. And I'll help you look for the underwear after this buzz wears off. Fair warning, it could be hours before I muscle through this, so you may want to get a head start on those posters."

And so it went. Anytime Husband had a beer, I had to watch. It's almost cataclysmically unfair, the alcohol balance that's struck between the impregnated and the impregnator. For social reasons and also not wanting to have her baby come out looking like that creature from *The Goonies*, the pregnant woman shies away from any and all alcoholic beverages. It's for nine long months, but it's also for the good of the little peep inside, so the mom sucks it up, burns her "Margaritas Make My Clothes Fall Off" t-shirt, and deletes all liquor store directions from her GPS, day planner, and Post-It Notes stuck under her car seat in case of the Zombie Apocalypse.

She forgets these places exist and, instead, does her best to deal with stress by practicing yoga, drinking green tea, or crying all day. Dealing with the day's trials by going to the bar like a normal person is simply out of the question. Not to mention, on top of the bonfire she's making of the most reliable ways to solve her anxiety, she also tosses her cigarettes, lighters, and any and all medication she may have been using as a backup plan to fall asleep. Unfortunately, NyQuil isn't a fall back option, even in the smallest of shot glasses, under the most watchful eye of the dog.

And while she knows she didn't get herself pregnant and it's not entirely fair that she has to give up her gin and tonics, she bids farewell to her Camel Lights and jumps on the greener, soy-laden Jack LaLanne train of clean living. She will do this to better herself. She will be healthier. Her baby will come out with both eyes facing forward, and, who knows, she may even live longer due to this nine-month-long detox. She is bold and brave, and after much self-resolution, has embraced this new lifestyle.

Three months in, the perks seem obvious, and the pregnant woman finds herself to be far more health-conscious than she'd originally thought possible. It begins to occur to her that, after she has this baby, her skin will glow like Jennifer Aniston's and she'll have the shining digestive tract of Gwyneth Paltrow. Did she even need alcohol before? No. Look what it'd been doing to her waistline. Look at her pallid skin and lack-luster nails and hair. Her hair had been practically falling out from all the gin and Houlihan's coasters she'd accidentally eaten out of nervous habit. Bars were places unhealthy people wanted to go, if they were trying to look like a sailor after a ship wreck, body mauled by a passing school of rabid tuna.

And then it dawns on her, the fact that all her friends need to stop drinking too, so they can feel as good as she's already talked herself into feeling. The next day, she'll waddle up to all her friends and let them know how she's discovered the key to their happiness, along with her own. No one needed cool, refreshing mojitos. All they needed was to band together and form a tribe that churned its own butter, grew its own carrots, and worked out to Zumba as a group. Happy hours were for the desperate, the needy, the whiners, and the people who wanted to have fun.

About the time the logic becomes circular and the pregnant woman realizes she's talked herself back into the bar, her husband validates this point by rolling out a giant keg in front of her, tapping it, and enjoying several hundred ice cold beers in front of her. Suddenly, she is reminded that she is the only person in the equation it took to make another person who can't have alcohol for nine months. And, while the husband half of the team kicks his feet up and makes love to that Bud Light, the impregnated begins to grow claws she never knew she had. And she must bury them deep within the sofa cushions so as not to drive them deep within the calf muscles of her beloved.

So begins the test: How many minutes can she stand being in the same room with him while he drinks? How many times can she hear, "You're a trooper," before she goes postal, rips out the glue gun, and builds a wall of cans, strictly to keep him from coming back through the front door? If he asked if she could get him another beer, is it really considered murder?

I jumped head-first into this particular brand of mental roulette. My "for better or worse" part of the vows—which had never really been test-driven past my love's affinity for leaving cabinet doors open so I'd run my face into them—finally got pulled out for a spin. The reason being that it wasn't only the fact that Husband was allowed to drink and I wasn't; it was everything that came with that fact.

Suddenly, I wasn't just the wife, I'd also been volunteered for a slew of other duties. Namely, taxi driver. It isn't enough that the woman must watch helplessly as her soul mate enjoys refreshing margaritas in the company of friends while she sits, lonely in her sober sombrero; she must also become the carpool mom of the bar scene. This phenomenon is far more pronounced in couples experiencing their first pregnancy, mainly because the new father hasn't developed his intuition enough to know that his life is in danger, and he may soon be afforded a one-way trip to meet his maker via pillow to the face in the wee hours of the morning. Only after he hears the distant calls of the angels will he stop to consider the fact that that last trip to the bar may not have been the most ideal choice.

Husband was no different than any of the other rookies. Too young to realize that I'd developed strangling powers which were only being restrained by the fact that I was way too tired to go out and find a replacement father before the babies showed up, he lived life in perfect oblivion. Sensing a golden opportunity that would last for months, he never hesitated to hand over the keys. "You don't mind, do you?"

"Nah. You know the steering wheel in your car? I love guessing whether I'll fit behind it or not."

"You sure you don't mind going out with everyone?"

I'd shake my head. "Are you kidding me? I love being the only sober one at parties. Who'll go around and refill all the napkin holders? Who'll make sure the bathroom always has toilet paper? No, it'd be pure chaos if I didn't go. Not to mention, who's going to start Trivial Pursuit? Those pie pieces won't just set themselves up."

Smiling, he'd hand over the keys. "You're such a trooper. That's what I love about you. You can still have fun, even though you're pregnant."

Cramming myself behind the wheel, I'd nod. "Well, I've always found 'fun' to be such a subjective term. Like, you can have 'fun' drinking, or have 'fun' learning to cross stitch with one hand."

And so it went. Did I always want to be the sober driver? No. Did I want to go to parties where I was the only one not having a polar-ice-cap-cold gin and tonic? No. But I also didn't want to sit at home either. There are only a few things that wait for a pregnant woman who punks out when everyone and their mother has decided to hit the town. Most of these things involve worrying, being sober, worrying some more, being sober, wondering if her significant other will make it home in one piece, being sober, looking at pictures of cats saying witty things, being sober, wishing she'd just bitten the bullet and gone out, being sober, starting a lame hobby like making piggy banks out of popsicle sticks, quitting said hobby when the glue gun almost catches the open bag of Doritos on fire, and realizing she could've been sober and out with other people instead of staring at the wall and wondering whether that crack that looks like a spider has always been there, or if it's an actual spider and she should move to the other couch.

It took me a few bouts of this logic before I started going out with Husband instead of staying home. I wasn't going to be lame, sitting at home watching leopards mate on the Discovery Channel. I'd go out. Be social. Live it up. Unfortunately, I regretted it every time.

The reality of leaving the house and wandering to the nearest bar in pursuit of a "regular" social life proved as easy as trying to fit in skinny jeans without the aid of a crowbar, Vaseline, and a personal trainer shouting, "Don't look down. Just pull." What my faulty logic had decided to omit was that the other half of not drinking while pregnant is that everyone else can. Everyone else in the world. Because you happen to be the only person pregnant at that particular moment in time. And once you step out of the door and into that melting pot of tipsy girls and cross-eyed guys, you're not only the only sober person within a fifty-mile range, you're also now the counselor, confessor, object of random prodding, and, if one is truly lucky, the drink watcher when everyone yells as a group, "Jimmy's going to tattoo himself."

Admittedly, I usually excelled at the position of counselor. Using my grown-up voice, I looked whoever it was in the eye and said, "No, I believe hooking up with the man who just tried to pay his tab with Monopoly money is a mistake."

"You're sure?"

"Yes."

A pair of sad eyes would search mine for wisdom. "But, he said he owned an entire railroad."

"Hmm. Does he also own a boardwalk?"

"How'd you know?"

"Lucky guess. We'll give you a ride home."

Or some such other likely scenario would pop up.

"I'm not sure why she broke up with me."

"Are you still playing *World of Warcraft* on twenty-four–hour intervals?"

"It's just a hobby."

"I see."

"Someday, I'll find someone who gets me."

"Probably. Like I always say, the perfect person will find you in your basement when the timing's right."

It wasn't all without reward, though. At the end of every pregnant bar outing, I always got to look forward to talking to myself while Husband slept peacefully beside me on the ride home. If he stayed awake, we'd trade stories about how funny everyone was, and I'd recount how many times I managed to not pee myself by accidentally waiting too long to go to the bathroom.

Husband would lead. "Wasn't Joe hilarious when he said he thought the bartender had tried to cut him off?"

I'd laugh jovially. "He *was* trying to cut him off. But did you see how I almost peed myself and was running with that Heineken glass under me for safety's sake? I tell ya. You and I are practically a modern-day Laurel and Hardy. By the way, we've gotta give Cindy a ride home because Joe tried to pick her up with Monopoly money again."

For me, it was no use pouting about how I couldn't drink and he could. All pregnant women have to suck it up, put on their big-girl pants, and accept the fact that they can't have a margarita for nine months. But, just when it all seems in vain, when one more thought of the spouse enjoying a festive fall beer during Oktober Fest makes you want to strangle him with a pair of lederhosen, the sun rises and brings with it no hangovers or swollen eyes or splitting headaches. No, the pregnant woman gets to massage her swollen ankles with a clear head, eat a horribly greasy breakfast because she wants to, and throw up—not because of a shaky stomach from a poorly chosen dozen Rock Lobster shots combined with chasers of Goldschlager, but because she's growing a person. So, clearly, not drinking has its perks. Babies also can't stand when people try to pay for things with Monopoly money. And no one wants to be kicked in the bladder for that.

6
Crying and Other Ways to Lighten the Mood

The post office was the first to alert me to the problem. After waiting on hold and listening to "The Star-Spangled Banner" several times, a voice popped on the line. "Post Office, how can we help you?"

I leaned on the kitchen counter and stared at the pile of envelopes. "Yes, I'd like to report an incident."

"Of course, ma'am, how can I help? You weren't flashed by one of the mail carriers were you?"

"Sadly, no. You see, my mail's soaking wet."

"Wet?"

I turned an envelope over in my hand. "Yes. I suspect it was given a bath before it was delivered. Now, I'm a sensible woman, and definitely understand the need to scrub *Hustler* with soap and water, but my electric bill's bleeding through my *Dog Owner Quarterly*. I'm not sure if I'm supposed to pay fifty dollars or electrocute my boxer." Exasperated, I laid my forehead on the counter.

"Ma'am?"

"Yes, mailman?" I whispered.

"Are you pregnant?"

"Yes."

"I see. Did you happen to watch a commercial of any kind on TV before going to get the mail?"

"Yes, it was about discounted oil changes. Fifty percent off, down at the Lube and G-G-G-Go. Did you know they just throw all that old oil away? Like it doesn't even matter?" A lump formed in my throat.

"Listen, ma'am, it's a common problem. We're always getting reports from pregnant women about soggy envelopes. I suggest you have your husband get the mail until that baby gets here."

"Thanks, mailman." Hanging up, I wiped off the phone, hung the bills out to dry, and reflected a moment. Crying? I didn't cry, especially about commercials. Paige Kellerman only cried at two things: funerals, and when *Angel* got canceled prematurely, leaving the series finale lacking and me wandering in search of a new *Buffy* spin-off, only to come up so, so short. One of my pregnancy manuals had warned about increased emotional sensitivity, but I'd simply assumed it was talking about Husband.

Crying? No, but there seemed to be an epidemic of everyone else being ridiculously annoying and irritating and redundant. When the guy in the drive-thru had forgotten the hot sauce, I'd reminded him and politely waited until he returned. When the solitary packet of "Flamin' Hot" dropped into my outstretched hand, climbing back through the drive-thru window, grabbing his collar, and shouting, "How's a woman supposed to cover twenty bean burritos with one packet of hot sauce?" seemed more than appropriate. Was it some kind of packet for a mouse who loves cheaply priced, not authentic Mexican food served after midnight? He handed me the extra pile of napkins to "dry my face," obviously trying to cover his tracks. Clearly, I was sweating from burrito anticipation, not crying. Had the man ever waited for a burrito? Pure torture. The news was inundated with stories of people dying at Chipotle in tragic bean-fight smotherings. Reporters were always quick to jump on the theory that a person waiting for pinto beans was a loose cannon.

Since I'd gotten pregnant, people in department stores, people in traffic, people breathing were insensitive. Did I need any help finding anything? Have a nice day? Would I like help out to my car? Not to mention, driving the car was a nightmare because people were constantly stopping at stoplights and merging in traffic.

One beautiful day, a man waved me in to the roaring traffic. I mouthed back, "It's because you feel sorry for me, isn't it? You heard I almost failed my driving test when I was fifteen, and thought you'd try to make me feel better about it. Well, I don't. And I'm stuck behind this steering wheel. And now you're using that off-ramp like this never happened."

Sales people weren't much better. "I can get you a fitting room and help you with sizing, if you'd like."

I bit my finger. "Are you saying someone as big as me couldn't possibly find a sweater large enough to cover all this? That someone shaped like a globe which has been meticulously made to scale shouldn't be touching your precious clothes?"

She backed away. "No, ma'am. I just thought maybe you'd like some assistance. You've been crying on the handbags for the last thirty minutes. That Coach bag just exploded."

"I don't have any money."

"We don't discriminate. For three hundred dollars, I'll pretend you didn't snot on the kate spade clutch."

It was perplexing. Coinciding strangely with my second trimester, puppies, butterflies, the way peanut butter could be so smooth, yet so creamy at the same time, all caused an odd reaction in my tear ducts. Desperate and convinced it was late onset adult allergies, I'd even put up a question about the topic on a pregnancy message board.

My Dear Gentlewomen,

I write only because I fear that the hay, the pollen, and some soft grasses have affected my fragile constitution, for I cannot but step outside before my bosom heaves, for sooth. What say ye?

Other pregnant women answered and insisted they were crying all the time, and felt solidarity in the fact that I was having the same problem with being overly-sensitive.

"When you broads are done having a pity party," I wrote back, "Can someone please weigh in about these pregnancy allergies? And you, 2Cute2Boot, no one wants to share lunch with you because you already admitted you eat their desert and then cry on yourself. Thanks, Paige."

Several days after the mail dried and still perplexed

about my condition, I decided to relax and watch a movie with Husband. He squeezed my hand. "What'll it be tonight?"

"Anything to take my mind off this crazy world. Let me pull both of my pizzas out of the oven before we start." After arranging my smorgasbord within arm's reach, pretzel bites at the ready, emergency Twix at my feet in case I got stuck and needed motivation to get up again, I settled into my spot, hit Play, and we started watching *Up*.

"Are you crying?"

I looked over and realized Husband was staring at me. "What? No, but there's an inordinate amount of jalapenos on this pizza. My eyes are watering more than the time you warned me not to come in the bathroom, but I charged in after my mascara anyway. Eyelashes just aren't that important."

He smirked. "It's okay if you are, you know, crying. It's a sad movie. Does it make you think of us? Is that why you're sniffing?"

"It makes me think I might punch you, but with lots of love, so it hurts but reassures you that I'll still iron your pants if you need to go anywhere nice. I won't have people thinking I let my man walk around all wrinkly."

"Whatever you say."

I watched the rest of the movie in silence. My soul mate accusing me of over-sensitivity made me want to slap a well-meaning sea lion right in the whiskers. Then again, the movie had been sad. Clearly, *Up* is someone's idea of a sick joke.

"Hey, Betty. Wanna watch an inspirational kid's movie about heroes viewed through a child's eyes, and the necessary adjustment of that lens during adulthood?"

"That sounds great, Jimmy. I'll get the popcorn and fountain drinks."

"By the way, a sweet little old lady dies in the first five minutes."

"Uh huh."

"And her husband becomes a recluse...There's also a possibility you won't want to live after you finish it."

Who were these animation people who got to put any old thing in a movie nowadays? Who makes a children's movie about two people falling in love, and then kills one of them off in a horrible "I got really old and died of natural causes" way? Probably the same people who'd call *Fargo* "the feel-good film of 1996."

One thing was for sure; there was definitely a correlation between stupid, sappy things and my corneas. For the next week, I dedicated all the hours I should've been working to writing letters to various medical specialists.

Dear Dr. Dan Hilger-Smith-Svenson-Collins DDS BA,

I hope this letter finds you doing well. The internet says you have the ability to fix sight and sell life insurance, if I ask. Please let me know if you'd be interested in taking on a special case study. I feel I have a rare eye condition which could use your expertise. My eyes won't stop watering. This tends to worsen when I watch the Sarah McLachlan commercial where she's trying to get rid of used dogs.

I'm not sure if it's the combination of the music, or the fact she's drawing and quartering my soul with her accusatory eyes, but she makes me feel like I kick Chihuahuas for a living. Before you ask, yes, I am pregnant. I only mention it because every other doctor thinks it's important to mention it when they tell me they can't help me. Looking forward to hearing back from you.

Regards,

Paige

After several weeks of over-active tear ducts, I couldn't take it anymore. Stumped, I decided to go back to what seemed to be the beginning of my problem. Ruling out the morning my tights cut off the circulation to my knee caps, television seemed to be the next logical conclusion. Determined to narrow down the cause of my sensitivity and put it in check, one Saturday evening, while the dog snored and Husband played video games, I beached myself on the couch and scrolled channels to see if I could find the thing which grew a lump in my throat and made my eyes water. Several passes at *Wheel of Fortune* and a close brush with trying to order a steam mop (an attempt crushed only by being too fat to make it to my wallet) later, I clicked randomly until I found a movie.

Thirty minutes into my experiment and crudely tested hypothesis, I heard Husband calling me. "Honey, you all right?"

I looked up. "Of course I'm all right. Why wouldn't I be? You didn't eat all my M&Ms, did you? Because we've talked about that. Ask first, and then you can have some.

But only the plain ones. The peanut are reserved for Sunday Afternoon Second Lunch."

"Uh, no. I asked because you're crying all over the remote. I thought I saw it sizzle a little bit. You'd tell me if you felt your heart skip slightly, wouldn't you?"

Looking down, I noticed my shirt had soaked through to my bra. "Well how about that?" I stared back at Husband. "I think I may have figured out what's wrong with my eyes. I'll get back to you." Turning back to the screen, I devoted every last ounce of energy I had, focusing on the potential key to my physical distress.

An hour later, I turned my blurry eyes back to Husband and shouted, "I've got it, you juicy cantaloupe of a man. It took me an hour and a half, but I know what's wrong with me."

Husband picked up the chair he'd knocked over when my scream sent him head-long into the dog bowl. His brow went up. "So you're ready to admit it?"

"Admit what?"

"You're crying because being pregnancy is making you emotional."

In an act of defiance, I re-adjusted my sleeping left boob. "I'll admit to crying and that I'm, perhaps, a tad emotional, but you shouldn't look so self-righteous, considering it's your fault."

"My fault? How can pregnancy hormones be my fault?"

I rolled forward. "Don't you try and blame our miracle. This movie's made it perfectly clear what's going on here."

"Wait, what are you watching?"

"*The Notebook*."

He ran his hand through his hair. "I don't get it."

"You wouldn't. It's possibly the greatest movie ever. God crafted it with His loving hands and sent it to Earth so that all women would not only adore Ryan Gosling dressed in old-timey garb, but also be inspired to write down their life stories in the event that they lost their memories and needed to hire someone to read it back to them."

"I still don't get it."

I thrust half an Oreo towards him. "All this time I thought I had adult-onset allergies, and it wasn't that at all. It's because you've never bothered to row me in a boat."

"Adult-onset what? Is that even a thing?"

"Don't change the subject."

"Are you trying to tell me you want me to put you in a boat? I can make some calls. I heard Angelina Jolie gave birth in a pool or something."

Waiving my arms, I made canoe motions. "No, you never rowed me in a boat, or built me a house, or…or made out with me in the rain and then gifted me a pre-dictable art studio I could sit naked in." I pulled the blanket over my head and slumped in a corner of the couch.

"But you don't even paint. And you hate nature."

"I know that."

"So you're crying because I never wanted you to paint? Would you settle for a beret with 'I'm a Mommy' on it?"

"I'm crying because you should've rowed me in a crappy row boat before you impregnated me. The movie said so. That boat will always be the asterisk on our relationship. I needed romance. Romance in a boat."

"I still think it's hormones. Is there anything I can do to make you feel better?"

"Yes."

"What's that?"

"Hit 'Replay' for me. I've rolled too far from the remote. And I need to see them crawl into bed and kick the bucket together again."

"Sure, and I promise to row you in a boat before our next baby."

"Will you fill it with burritos?"

"Anything for you."

7

The Only Way That Baby Is Getting Out Is on a Yoga Ball

Somewhere around the five-month mark, it occurred to me that, with all the time I'd spent eating, I hadn't put much thought into how the babies would eventually make their way into the world. As a child, I'd heard babies find a way through the gift shop, and out of the womb via the belly button. And if they made it out successfully, they got a cigar of their choice. Something about that information seemed inaccurate. There was no way a gift shop could fit in a uterus. So, oatmeal creme pie in hand, I sat down and asked Google how it thought I should get my babies out when the time came.

The keywords "baby" and "exit" spirited me to science websites littered with diagrams, stick figures, and objects flying out of saloon doors. Using coal as a medium, I sketched down what seemed most important. And, with my best handwriting, I carefully labeled the sections, wrote my name on it so no one would steal it to get their baby out first, and stuck it in my pocket. Shortly after, I dialed the doctor's office. "Hello. Yes, I'd like to make an appointment. An emergency? No, but I'd like to cross-reference some research with you. Otherwise, these babies might get stuck. Did I what? Oh, I'm not in labor. Why? What does that look like? Are there balloons? Someone on the internet mentioned balloons."

The nurse sighed, penciled me in for my monthly appointment, and hung up. For the next few days, I spent my time thinking of questions. Would gravity do most of the work? If I didn't know where it was, would the secret trapdoor open on its own, or would I need a password? Was the password "baby," or something more covert like "the antelopes gallop at midnight." If the babies didn't come out on the due date, would they renew their lease for another nine months? Did my insurance policy cover spontaneous combustion?

A week later, list in hand, I set up camp in one of the tiny exam rooms and waited for the mysteries of the universe to be explained. After several minutes of briefing myself on avoiding the dangers of Lyme disease, I heard a soft knock, and my new doctor bounced into the room. Setting down the pamphlet, I sat at attention and nodded. "I'm so glad you're here. We have some things to go over."

She beamed at me. "Mrs. Kellerman, how are you today? The nurse told me you had some questions. I didn't see anything that concerned me on your charts. What seems to be the problem?"

I poked my belly. "Well, I'm fairly certain how they got in there, but I don't know how to get them out."

"Out?"

"Yes. Oh great, I've confused you, too. Hold on." I dug in my pocket and handed her the list. "Ok, so I looked up some ideas on the internet. If we put our heads together, we may be able to come up with something."

"Is this coal?"

"I was out of oil paint. Listen, by my calculations, gravity will probably be on our side, but like I always say, 'Always be prepared, most of the time.' So put your thinking cap on."

She took my hands off her shoulders. "Mrs. Kellerman, I've delivered hundreds of babies. And I can assure you it'll be fine. I do have a suggestion, though."

"Before you say anything, I already researched those special Chechnian birth monkeys. Way out of our price range. Did you know they'll even make you hot tea?"

"I was thinking more along the lines of a birthing class."

"Oh."

"They'll go through all the steps with you."

"Can you rent the birth monkeys from them?"

"There aren't any monkeys, but I think you'll feel better."

After taking down the website she suggested, I bid my good doctor adieu, sped home, and pulled out my computer. The class description delighted me:

Figured out how to get that baby in there, but don't know how to get it out when it's time? We're your people! Just take out a second mortgage on your home and come join us. Our trained instructor will take you through the vast labyrinth that is pregnancy. We love dumb questions, confused expressions, and women as big as whales.

You will need: a pillow, a fair amount of bladder control, and the father (or a good friend who doesn't mind when you scream and throw things).

Cost: How much is in your checking? A dollar more than that.

They seemed on the level, so I clicked "I'm desperate. Sign me up!" and went in search of a decent pillow.

"I don't see why this is necessary." Husband took the keys out of the ignition.

I wriggled out of the passenger seat and opened the back door. "Unless you want to catch these babies on our bathroom floor, we need this class. They'll teach us how to do it the right way."

"I guess so."

"Okay then, grab a pillow and let's go. Don't take the squashy one. I'm assuming part of the curriculum is nap-time, and I'll need the good one if I'm going to get any rest."

Clutching our bed things, we padded into the brick building, ran a maze of corridors, and finally found a room with a sign on the door: "Birthing Class: Must Be This Fat to Enter." I brightened. "I'm that fat, honey. We're here."

Another frightened-looking couple opened the door and let us in. I nodded. "Thanks. Your baby stuck up there, too?" They filed in behind us and we made our way to the sign-in sheet, where we were greeted by the instructor.

"Hey, guys! Just put down your names and take one each of the fifty brochures I set out."

My pillow plopped to the ground, and I began loading Husband with paper. After a few minutes, I peeked through the stack. "Can you breathe?"

"Yeah."

"Good, because that was only the first twenty-five. There are two more piles of welcome literature, and one that looks like it might be about how to give birth upside down."

I was on my nineteenth pick, a pamphlet about how storks didn't bring babies, when our instructor piped up. "Okay, now everyone find a seat and we'll get started. Oh, and remember to grab a yoga ball before you sit down." While Husband tried to file our paper stack under his seat, I waddled over to the yoga balls, nabbed one, and rolled it over to our seats. By the time I plopped down, things had gotten started. The anticipation was palpable.

The instructor clapped her hands and pointed at the circle. "Let's go around, say our names, and a little bit about ourselves. I'll start. I'm Shelly, I'm not pregnant, and how skinny I am right now makes you want to hit me in the face with your yoga balls." She smiled and nodded at a timid redhead to her right. "Now you guys."

Like a deer in front of a Jeep, the woman stared and stuttered. "I-I'm Angie, and this is Dave. We think we're having a baby. I mean, we're having a baby and it's a boy, and—"

Dave chimed in. "Yeah, a baby."

Good job, Dave.

The next couple just stared and drooled on themselves. The pair after them answered "What are you having?" with "I think it's a walrus."

My chest relaxed. These people were as clueless as I was. Finally, Shelly turned in our direction. "And what about you guys?"

My hand shot up. "He did it, but that's as far as we've gotten. Well, that and the fact that there are two probably strikingly good-looking babies in there. So, let's jump to the part when they start knocking and want to come out. What type of baseball mitt would you suggest? Rawlings? I hear the leather's nice and flexible."

"Um."

I backtracked. "You're right, that was dumb of me. You obviously gave us the yoga balls because we've got to 'bounce' the babies out, correct? Can I take mine home for practice? There's a lot of clenching and unclenching I need to run through."

"We'll get to that."

"Ok, Shelly, but time is of the essence."

That first night, our confused group was led through a diagram of body parts and instructed to take note of the "chute" the babies would be exiting from. The yoga balls, we were informed, were for our comfort. If we needed to take stress off our backs, we could either sit on the ball, or have our partner roll us onto it like graceful beluga whales.

Elbows propped on my big blue sphere, I raised my hand at the end of class. "Shelly?"

"Yes?"

"The pictures are really nice, but I'm still short an exit strategy."

"We'll talk more about that next time, and even watch a video of the real thing. You guys have a nice evening."

I flopped off the ball. "A video, huh? Sounds good. Although, audio book also sounds like a solid option."

Unfortunately, for the next few classes, we were led along like sheep:

Week 2—Your Baby: How it got in there

Week 3—Diapering: Your baby won't come out potty trained

Week 4—Fat Jokes: How to shrug it off without throwing bricks through windows.

By the time I waddled into week five's class, I was sure I'd been duped out of my money. At the end of week four, the instructor had told us to get ready for the video, but still hadn't delivered. With a heavy heart, I rolled onto my yoga ball, noted the wheezing and slightly panicked noise it made, and scanned the room. Redhead looked about as frustrated as I did, but I suspected it was because her husband was ignoring the fact that her ankles were as big as oil rigs and she was having trouble propping them on her ball.

Shelly bounced in. "Evening, class, how are we doing tonight?"

I made the universal sign for "fat and slightly disgruntled" by snorting and heaving myself into my plastic chair, a detestable piece of furniture I'd noticed shrinking over the past five weeks, and executed the ankle prop Red had been struggling with. I was Mary Lou Retton waiting for a ten and someone to rub my hip fat.

Our instructor looked around the circle composed of

suffering faces and stifled gas. "Tonight we'll be watching the birth video. Now, it may be a little much, but when the actual birth happens, I'll warn you so you can look away."

I wondered why I'd I want to look away. Finally, we were getting somewhere. The very answers to the cosmos could be in what we were about to watch. The plot unfolded. Columbo was about to ask the final question. The anticipation that had built inside me wanted desperately to jump out and declare, "Mrs. Peacock in the kitchen with the pipe!"

Husband scooted next to me and whispered, "Here we go."

I dug into the pile of peanut butter crackers I'd grabbed on the way in. "Yep. And yay to movie night. After this, we should know everything we need to."

"Uh huh."

Over the next thirty minutes, what we witnessed can be summed up as such:

See Tammy. See Tammy look like she'd rather be doing anything other than wrestle a watermelon. Look how Tammy yells and moans like a cat stuck in a dryer. There's Tom. Tom got Tammy pregnant. Look and see Tom hiding under the bed. See Tom trying to escape to the vending machines? Silly Tom.

See Tammy roll on the yoga ball. Where's Tom? Tom just got slapped in the face for trying to touch Tammy. Bad Tom. See Tom trying to be more supportive. See Tammy throw the bed pan at Tom. See Tammy bring down curses upon the entire room. Hear the screams of Tammy as she punches the nurse. Look, look. See, see. Here comes a miracle.

The miracle looked strikingly like my hand in front of my face.

Husband whispered in my ear again. "You don't want to see?"

"I can't. It's horrifying. That's not a trapdoor, it's a bowling ball trying to come out a coin slot. Maybe Shelly needs to check the movie. I think she started *Aliens* instead."

"I think it's fairly accurate."

"You would."

When the lights came on, I looked out from between my fingers. Redhead had squeezed Dave's hand off. Poor handless Dave, catching his newborn daughter had just gotten twice as difficult. A couple who hadn't said anything for the past four weeks were holding hands, rocking back and forth and staring at something in the distance I could only assume was a land where watermelons cascaded out of the smallest hole in the world. A dark-haired woman in the corner was mumbling and sprinkling crushed crackers on her head.

Shelly looked around the shell-shocked troop. "Ok, so what did you think?"

I raised my hand. "I think the lady with crackers could use a Dirt Devil."

She smiled. "I know that was a lot to take in. You guys have any questions?"

"Yes, um, do you think Tammy and Tom are still together? I think she may have stabbed him with her IV towards the end there. Oh yeah, and where was the trap-door? I must've missed it when I used my Husband's shirt to try and wipe my corneas out of existence."

"Trapdoor?"

"You know. The secret door? The password? Open sesame, blah, blah, blah? All I just saw was a lot of scream-ing. And possibly Tom's murder."

She shuffled her tennis shoes. "Well, in your case, it'll probably be a little different."

I breathed a sigh of relief. "Ahh, so it'll be one of those old-timey things. Knock me out, hand me the baby when I come to? I'll make sure and put on some makeup, so when I look surprised and shout, 'What, a baby for me?' it'll look good in the album. Which reminds me. Do you know anyone who scrapbooks professionally?"

"You're having twins, so there's a good possibility you'll be having a C-section. That's where they take the babies out surgically. Uh, Mrs. Kellerman?"

But I couldn't hear her. I was too busy rocking back and forth, sprinkling crackers over my head with the lady in the corner. From what I gather from Husband, the only thing I said as he dragged me out by my feet was, "Birth monkey."

8
Cankles

My night's sleep had been unbearable. It could've been Husband ripping off my covers and trying to wrap himself like a mummy at two in the morning, or the dog licking the bed skirt and pooping out a new duvet on the sweater regrettably left on the floor, but there'd been something else. Something like two pigs engaged in a wrestling match at the bottom of the bed. That made me angry. There was only one pig in the house, and that was me. No more pigs need apply. After all, who'd slept next to the last of the cheesecake? If someone was after the cheesecake, things were about to get uglier than the hair on my legs from January to mid-April.

Husband growled and pulled the covers over his ears. "You'll have to get through me first, buddy."

Seeing that I'd have to investigate myself, I took courage in everything Nancy Drew ever taught me as a child, and, using the headboard as leverage, hoisted my seven-months' pregnant self to a sitting position. Delicately, I pulled back the covers, and stared. Inching my fingers over, I tapped Husband's back. "Honey, you need to see this."

"I married her because she promised not to eat all the chips. She lied."

"Honey, wake up."

Finally, he rolled over. "What is it? Are you hungry again?"

I pointed to the foot of the bed. "I think you need to do something."

"What do you mean?"

Grabbing his hand, I whispered, "I'll distract them while you get the bat. When they're not looking, hit them in the head."

"Hit what in the head?"

"The aliens. Go, now, before it's too late."

"Those are your ankles."

I shook his shoulder. "Listen, while you're dillydally-ing, those things are making their way up here to eat both our faces off. Did we learn nothing from watching Ripley fight for her life...twice?"

Horrified, I watched him roll back over and go back to sleep, leaving me to face the things that'd formerly been my ankles. I wiggled my feet. Lazily, the two bar-rels clunked together and rolled, lamely, to the side. What had been delicately tapered stems when I'd fallen asleep now looked like twin Goodyear blimps advertising my immobility. Nancy Drew didn't know the half of it. At least, I was sure I'd never stumbled upon *The Mystery of Shadow Ranch's Cankle Cow Show*. Then again, maybe that had been in Bess's spin-off series.

While getting ready for work, I did my best not to look at what had, hours before, been calves separate from ankles, ankles separate from feet. Gazing down was like having free tickets to a rodeo. Someone was going to have to wrestle those two fat calves into submission, and, sadly, I'd never even ridden a horse.

For the first time in my pregnancy, shoes became a problem. I sat in front of my closet and deliberated, finally settling on a pair of black flip flops. The snow outside suggested this was a terrible idea, but the high heels I'd initially chosen had cut off circulation, caused my body to turn a lovely shade of violet, and knocked me out. After I'd clawed my way back to consciousness, I didn't really care what I wore on my feet. So, like a pregnant Ninja Turtle, I waddled to the car and drove to work.

The day was more or less a blur of cankle destruction. My boss was sweet enough to call attention to the condition early, so everyone could stare at their convenience.

"Hi."

Taking off my headset, I looked up. "Hello."

"So, you're wearing flip flops."

"I am. I know it's not exactly dress code, but I don't have any shoes left that fit."

She crossed her arms. "They're just so big."

"Umm, what?"

"Your ankles. They're huge."

"I know."

By then, the rest of the department had gathered round. I was blanketed in whispers and gestures symbolizing big, round things. At the back of the mob, a guy held up a sign: "Cankles Go Home."

My boss laughed. "It's just, they're so big.

I shifted in the swivel chair too quickly. One of my enormous ankles hit the wall, started a shock wave, and knocked over a row of computers. "Real big."

"Well, I just wanted to let you know."

"Thanks for that."

Unfortunately, my boss wasn't the worst thing to happen that morning. Two hours later, the right cankle, left unattended, strayed on my way to the bathroom, caught a phone cord, and almost choked a man to death. After filling out the proper HR paperwork for nearly causing the untimely demise of a co-worker, I made it to the lunch room just in time to take out the pasta cart, smash the cash register to pieces with ankle bones the size of cantaloupes, and prompt the janitor to ask if I needed him to "whack those things with a stick" so they'd leave me alone.

After a long day of embarrassment, my swollen stems showed no mercy. On the way home from work, I noticed the car accelerating at an unusual rate. Just as my speed hit two hundred miles per hour, I realized my right cankle, which had grown to the size of a baby elephant, was trumpeting wildly and mashing down on the gas so hard that I'd successfully made it back to nineteen fifty-two, reset the clock, and left Doc Brown wondering what exactly a cankle was.

I cracked all the stairs on my way to the kitchen, waddled to the sofa, sat down, and, for the next hour, watched a Discovery Channel special on hunting cankles in the wild. In his jungle wear, the host jumped around, poking at a cankle that had been maimed and left to fend for itself.

"Now remember, I'm a trained professional," he bellowed. "A fine specimen. It looks harmless, but turn your back, and it can kill you. This one's headed for a reserve. If you ever run into a cankle by accident, please call a professional right away." A number appeared at the bottom of the screen: 1-800-canklecatch.

Husband got home about the time I realized my left ankle had settled on and was, subsequently, crushing the dog to death. As I propped my heels on the coffee table, the dog gave a wheeze of relief and crawled to safety.

"Hi." My skinnier half sat down and gave me a kiss. "How was your day?"

I shrugged. "Pretty good, if the city had requested destruction by thunderous, Godzilla ankles."

"I don't even know what you're talking about. They look fine. Hey, what time do you want to head to the engagement party?"

The table groaned as I rolled my feet towards Husband's questioning face. Dressing up wasn't exactly a priority; on a scale of Elephant Man to Joan Rivers, my sexy was lingering somewhere around a sleep-deprived Nicolas Cage, but I'd already sent the positive response that, yes, we'd bring our shining faces to his cousin's engagement party. "Let's go at half past naptime and a sandwich."

"Seven?"

"Okay. But there will still be a sandwich. Maybe if

I eat, these enormous legs will forget the feud they've sworn on the rest of my body."

Several sandwiches later, and after doing eight laps around a posh-looking neighborhood to kill time, we found ourselves in front of a beautiful home with hoards of skinny, beautiful people filing into it. I looked down. By aid of Turtle Wax and a crowbar, I'd managed to squeeze both feet into animal-print flats. It wasn't so much fashion forward as a realistic recreation of two obese leopards engaged in a battle to the death, via slapping each other in the face.

On the walk up the driveway, I pulled my black maxi dress down as far as it would go. If I had to wear shoes, the best I could do was pair them with yards of billowing fabric to envelope the mass they contained, and confuse people into thinking I was Morticia Addams. Instead of looking at my elephant feet, maybe everyone would think it was a costume party, give me candy, and let me be on my way.

Having successfully squeezed through the side door, and dragging a Formosa bush that'd caught on an ankle bone when I traipsed up the pathway, I followed Husband into a deliciously decorated living room, and was relieved to see it had finished making love to Pottery Barn long enough to host the party.

My cankles clumped over to the gleaming mini-bar-equipped beverage table, where I grabbed a bottled water and scanned the crowd of attractive people standing amidst polished tables and Scotchguarded couches. A young, blond girl was finishing a conversation with an impossibly handsome guy. She waived a slender hand in the air as her silver voice tinkled across the apple-scented air. "So then I said, 'Of course my ankles are so thin, I'm part gazelle.'"

I stayed frozen there just long enough to hear the wood floor crack beneath me. Waddling off the spot before I could drop through to the basement, I migrated to a group of Husband's family and decided to camp out. "Hey, guys."

His oldest sister looked me over. "You look cute."

I wiped the drool from the corner of my mouth. "Thanks. You guys look great." And skinny. Both of Husband's sisters and one of his cousins were pictures of beauty and slender ankles strapped into mile-high stilettos. His brother smiled at me. "You're really looking pregnant. How are you fee—" But a monstrous sound stopped him. "What was that? Did anyone hear thunder?" For a moment, the group debated whether a vicious, Midwestern storm was coming.

Blushing, I lifted the hem of my dress a few inches. "No, that's just the sound of my ankles slapping together. Either that, or a couple of adult seals are wrestling in what I presume is the dining room."

Aghast, several sets of eyes migrated to where my feet were nervously shuffling and taking on water. His cousin's mouth dropped open. "Oh my gosh, your feet. I mean, your ankles. I mean, you had ankles when we first met, right?"

I nodded. "They're really swollen." But they weren't just swollen. While I wasn't looking, they'd graduated to the size of shiny Christmas hams, hams Bob Cratchit would've been proud to drag home to his family and cause Tiny Tim to forget he was crippled. For a moment, I considered screaming "Jingle Bells" and waddling out of the room. But I was cornered, the panelists already firing questions.

"How'd they get like that?"

I leaned into the microphone. "I think the babies migrated to my ankles."

"Do they hurt?"

My shoes started splitting. "Only when I'm walking upright. Next question. Yes, you in the back."

"Will they affect your decision to run in next week's marathon?"

"I don't believe in exercise."

"If they get any bigger, what's your course of action?"

"I'm hoping I can tap them like a keg. I've made several inquires to local breweries who'll do it for a fee." Dress securely draped around ankles, I backed up and did my best to blend into the rich mahogany of the cabinets.

After my feet had been shown to several more inquiring aunts and uncles, and the mother of the groom had been assured that no one had let a wild elephant in her bathroom, despite the sound of porcelain cracking, I dragged my two barrels back to the car. Husband opened my door and I rolled in with a relieved sigh.

He patted my leg. "That was fun."

"Uh huh. I told you they were huge."

"You're beautiful."

I pulled out my cell phone and started punching buttons.

"Who're you calling?"

"The Discovery Channel." I shrugged. "I figured I'd call the 1-800-canklecatch people. They probably won't be able to beat these enormous cankles into submission, but they might be interested to see the toilet my ankles just knocked over and cracked in half. I think the general public is tired of hearing about the Pyramids. It's time to embrace the other half of reality television. The part where women with giant legs get let loose in a Williams-Sonoma. Chaos ensues. Pewter rabbits run for their lives."

"I still think you're beautiful."

"Can my cankles sleep on your side of the bed to-night?"

"No."

Fortunately, my cankles eventually went away after I gave birth. But I still keep a bat by my side of the bed. Just in case. In the time since this story was written, three people have been mugged by cankles, two cankles bit a friend of mine, and my favorite pair of leopard-print flats have been laid to rest. May they find the peace they deserve and never come in contact with killer cankles ever again.

9
The Night Avenger

The general public may not be aware, but it should be noted that the pregnant woman fears the night more than she does a rogue hemorrhoid. One would think that the nighttime would be the Holy Grail for the expectant, a deliciously relaxing time to bury herself in a cave of feathery duvets, hibernate until dawn, and use puddles of her own drool to mark the his-hers line in the bed. But, alas, the night only aggravates the condition, and causes mothers to sprout more hair on their backs, howl at the moon, and watch reruns of *Full House* until the sun comes up. I didn't realize exactly how much sleep I was losing until I got hit in the back of the head.

Padding down the driveway to get the paper one Saturday morning, I felt something slimy hit me. I wiped the old piece of apple core off, just in time to realize I needed to duck. After grabbing my belly and rolling behind the trashcan, I saw eight banana peels and a half-eaten pear whiz by my face. "Get the hell outta there," a voice shouted.

I peeked round the corner, just far enough to see one

of our elderly neighbors winding up to throw an old copy of O magazine my way. I held out my hand. "Hey, Bill, could you stop that?"

"Get outta my trashcan, you filthy animal."

Had I spooned with the dog last night because I was too lazy to find a blanket? Yes. Did it warrant being called an animal on my own property? No. "Hey, it's me, Paige. I live here, remember?"

He shuffled to the end of the driveway. "You get out of there, you dirty raccoon."

"I'm not a raccoon, Bill. I bathe my paws and a few things I eat, occasionally, but that's beside the point."

"Raccoons can't talk. Is this one of your dirty raccoon tricks?"

I shifted my weight and inched around the can. "I'm your neighbor."

He raised the magazine. "If you ain't a raccoon, why you got them circles around your eyes? Seems I should hit you with this magazine."

"If you're going to hit me, I'd rather you do it with a local paper, community is so important."

"Wait, I know you. You're the lady always jogs to the trash in her pajamas."

"Guilty. And they're actually sweat pa—"

"Better get them circles checked out, girl. No one's gonna want to marry ya like that."

At breakfast later that week, I questioned Husband. "Do I have circles?" I pressed the cold cereal spoon to my right eye.

"Is it that time of the month?"

"What? No, from not sleeping."

He kept his eyes on the paper. "You look as rested as the next person."

"I'm sitting next to a picture of Steve Buscemi."

"No one told you to buy that calendar."

I didn't really need Husband to tell me I was tired. I just hadn't realized it was starting to catch up to me so badly. Later that morning, I examined myself in the mirror. Big, black bags hung under each eye, drooped down my stomach, and grazed the floor. While I glued them back to my face with toothpaste, I reflected.

Not being able to sleep was something I hadn't anticipated. The stupid cartoon lady on the front of my birthing book looked like she slept twelve hours a night. Maybe sleeping was easier when your belly was drawn on, your pajamas were made of Laser Lemon crayon, and your hair resembled a quickly sketched Viking helmet. What was she giving birth to anyway, a paper chain of little Dutch kids holding hands?

Once my belly had reached the size of a toaster, sleep was out of the question. Insomnia blindsided me like the bus from *Speed*, Sandra Bullock flatting my rest with a flourish and carefully cultivated sweat and anxiety. At first I ignored it and tried to count sheep. But I started fantasizing about hunting them with a shovel, and Husband got tired of me whispering in his ear, "Bah, the sheeps is all in da pen," at three in the morning. Consequently, I turned to wandering the house instead.

Being up all night by one's self seems like it'd be boring, because it is. In an effort to combat my newly discovered boredom, I developed a routine consisting of time-sucking activities designed to help me make it until morning. There are, roughly, twelve billion hours between the time you go to bed and sunrise. If these hours aren't filled by the pregnant woman, with something passably interesting, she resorts to walking the halls, clanking chains, and looking for the long-lost bagel she'll never be able to retrieve from under the chaise lounge.

Late-night brainstorming delivered me mostly harmless activities, like crawling head-first into the cabinets in search of any cookies that might've escaped my wrath during Second Dinner. I'm convinced most people who think they have a poltergeist problem probably just have a stray pregnant lady stuck in their pantry, wedged behind the unopened boxes of caramel corn and shunned cans of French-cut green beans.

After eating everything that wasn't nailed down, and testing all the creaky spots in the floor to make sure there were still eighty-two and a half ways our house was folding in on itself, it was time to make my way to the couch and begin the night's lineup of TV fodder, available for everyone who's got another person or two living next to their bladder. Thankfully, whoever programs night television realizes that mothers and their unborn children love *Cops*.

While everyone else in the neighborhood was lost in REM sleep, I rocked back and forth and vicariously busted crack houses, chased half-naked perps over fences, and made handcuffs out of construction paper. I turned myself into a self-appointed neighborhood watch, and, one night after my adrenaline had gotten the better of me, ended up calling the police.

"Police, what's your emergency?"

"I'd like to report a disturbance."

"Yes, ma'am, how can we help you?"

"I've watched every episode of *Cops* and now I'm really bored. Do you think you can send an officer out to arrest someone and tape it? Nothing too serious, a crazed crackhead who's also a great candidate for *Hoarders* would be ok. We could transition from the arrest to an intervention."

After the chief promised not to have me arrested if I swore not to call again, I switched over to reruns of *Full House* and infomercials. By most sunrises, I'd not only learned a valuable life lesson, but could sell anything to anyone. Don't sneak a horse into the living room? Check. Realize that Uncle Joey's combination of tennis shoes and puppets made him look like he was one bad date away from *To Catch a Predator*? Yep. Accept the fact that everyone needs a Shark Steamer? Absolutely. People who didn't have one were living in squalor. Also, how had I been leaving the house without dusting my face with Bare Minerals? I was lucky someone hadn't thrown a rock at my head by now.

One morning, Husband padded downstairs on his way to the car. "Did you even go to sleep last night?"

"No."

"Are you gonna be okay if I go to work?"

"There's no time."

He leaned against the wall. "Time for what?"

I splashed some leftover soda on my eyes and slicked my bangs to the side. "If you don't act now, you may not have time to make me breakfast."

"I don't have time to make you breakfast."

"What if I said I only wanted a bagel and some juice?"

"Gotta go."

"If you get me a glass of milk, you don't have to get the bagel. And, if you act now, I'll throw in some steak knives, a cutting board, and some comfortable but chic lounge wear."

The garage door opened. "I love you. Don't play with knives. I'll see you tonight."

I waddled over and squeezed him. "Okay, just remember that I'm letting you take the car because I trust you. If any of your friends try to get you to hot rod on the way to school, don't be afraid to say no. Your uncles and I love you."

"What are you talking about?"

Staring into space, I patted him on the shoulder. "You know. I love you, Stephanie. It's just that I trust you, not other people."

"I don't know. And what are you staring at?"

I shook my head. "I'm waiting for the music. They always play music at this part."

At that, Husband kissed me on the forehead and left for work.

By the tenth week of no sleep, I was willing to try anything to get some rest. I drank warm milk, tried to hypnotize myself by watching a squirrel swinging with reckless abandon back and forth on the birdfeeder, and attempted to create the soothing sounds of rain by having Husband stand next to me shaking a bottle of water. I even tried to run a marathon, until I was dragged from the starting line on the grounds I'd reroute the runners who'd think I was an enormous pylon.

The weight from my huge stomach stopped any hope of lying on my back, side, or attempting to sleep standing up, something I'd tried, but Husband had objected to. The exact reasons escape me, but the man does have an irrational fear of being stared at while I sing him to sleep, using only the lower range of my humming repertoire. For the last few weeks of my pregnancy, I resorted to sleeping on the couch. Something which involved sitting up straight and talking to the flowered arm of my only confidant. "So, how was your day?"

"The dog farted on me right before I realized I've got a hole starting in my far right lining."

"That sounds terrible. I haven't slept in four months."

"Wow, that's pretty rough."

"You enjoy the living room?"

"I do. I'm a couch."

"You sure? I'm getting really heavy. I thought I heard your springs give out, the other night."

"No, man. Things are good."

"You wouldn't lie to me?"

"Listen, this gig is working out. I mean, you toss and turn a lot, but one of my cousins, he's a recliner in a Nebraska Furniture Mart...you know that place?"

"Yeah, I almost power-walked myself to death there,

last week. Then I cried on a really expensive bed."

"Well, my cousin says he gets sat on by people with way worse gas than you, so I keep it all in perspective."

"Thanks, couch."

"Anytime."

"Couch?"

"Yes, Paige?"

"You're all right."

From the bottom of my heart, I wish I could tell every pregnant woman I meet that I discovered the answer to getting sleep in the first, second, and third trimesters, but the truth is, I can't. Which is why yet another Saturday morning found me waddling back to the trashcan. Just as I opened the lid, Bill happened back out of his doorway. "Oh, it's you again. Takin' out the trash?" he asked.

I shook my head. "No, Bill. I'm going to climb inside, curl up next to that nasty orange peel lounging on that filthy Kleenex box, and try to get some sleep. If it works for the raccoons, I just might have a chance."

He shrugged, nodded, and closed the lid for me on his way back inside.

10
Maternity Leave and Other Ways They Tried to Kill Me

When my boss found out I was pregnant, it didn't take long for the questions to start. I knew it would happen. Shortly after the positive on the pregnancy test, I'd checked the employee manual for clauses containing anything along the lines of, "You will be required to have your baby on the floor of the cubicle. If birth will take longer than fifteen minutes, please notify your supervisor immediately for an extension. Please note: lunch hour may have to be forfeited." But, as I didn't find anything of the sort, I knew maternity leave was on the table. I just didn't know that the difficulty of the process would be similar to convincing the public I was the new face of Chanel.

Luckily, my supervisor started the grand inquisition before I could hem and haw about the issue too long. She tapped her newly manicured nails on the desk. "So, how're you feeling?"

I took my blanket off, rubbed my cankles, and set

aside a copy of *I'm feeling Fat and Tired—Collector's Edition*. "Good. You?"

"You know, I didn't get much sleep last night. Back pains and all. Just count yourself lucky you don't know how uncomfortable that can be." She considered something in the air in front of her. "I often think to myself, 'If someone has to do it, Veronica, old girl, it might as well be you who bears the suffering of the world,' and I grin and bear it. But, I don't like to talk about it much, not wanting to draw attention to how strong I am." The air around her suddenly cleared and her head poked through the self-important fog. "So, you're pregnant."

Hesitating in case it was a trick question, I nodded.

"Are you coming back after you have the, um…"

"Pack of Russian circus folk I'm carrying? Nope, they said they're not coming out until they get a raise, and finally get top billing over the tightrope-walking elephant." My diversion techniques needed work. "Oh, you meant the babies? Yep, I'll be coming back."

Her sigh of relief ruffled the papers on my desk. "Well, good. I guess that means you'll be applying for maternity leave then?"

"Do I have to write an essay?"

"No."

"That's good."

"I actually don't know what's involved in the whole process. I hear it's pretty complicated though."

"That's bad."

Like a crisp, unhelpful wind, she disappeared and left me staring at the computer. So, I didn't have to deliver the babies under my desk? Definitely a positive. Unfortunately, I was about to put on my maternity pirate hat and sail into unknown waters of complication. Blanket wrapped securely around shoulders, I hopped on the company website and started looking for some sort of roadmap to maternity leave.

My first search brought up eight helpful documents on why I was bothering to look for leave information, in addition to a questionnaire on who the father was, in case someone needed to be fired or promoted—that part wasn't clear. Subsequent searches pulled a file on what to do if your co-worker started a fire in his trashcan, a bulletin on hand washing before handing out office birthday cake, and a roughly scanned manual on how to fire people, using interpretive dance as a medium. Finally, after asking every person in the building, the janitor I cornered in the bathroom pointed me back to my boss. Back I waddled. "Do you know who I'd talk to first about leave?"

She blinked at me. "I think her name starts with an R, Rutabaga or something like that."

"Thanks, do you have an email for her?"

"What's email?"

"I'll figure it out."

One of my co-workers, no doubt pitying the pregnant girl chasing her tail, eventually slipped me the name and email address I needed. And, as it turns out, this particular HR person wasn't a vegetable. She was also extremely nice, which was great because she had a lot of confusing things to tell me about why what I was getting ready to do was as simple as getting Adam Sandler to stop making movies.

I hadn't worked much with HR, or Human Resources, for those who've never had the pleasure, but what I did know was its primary function was to take the standard time for any process and add a century to it. I'd once heard a guy requested time off to take care of some personal business, and, by the time HR got back to him, he'd been promoted, demoted, promoted again, and given a retirement party. The cake they sent him off with read "We've approved your request for leave." However, the first email I got back was hopeful:

> *Dear Paige,*
>
> *Congratulations on the babies. I'll be sending you instructions on what you need to do to request leave as soon as I find them. You haven't seen a manila envelope lying around, have you? Haha... just kidding...sort of.*
>
> *Sincerely,*
>
> *Cindy*

The second message simply read:

> *Dear Paige,*
>
> *Please see attachment.*
>
> *Cindy*
>
> *P.S. Please don't be mad.*

Why would I be mad? Cindy was only trying to help me. I clicked the document. A quick aside, if a file's size ever warns that the contents of an attachment exceed that of the unabridged version of *David Copperfield*, delete it, or enjoy the phone book someone just gifted you. When the introduction flashed on the screen, it was sizable but seemed straightforward.

Welcome, user. If you have found this page because you're pregnant, hit "continue." If you got here because you're looking for the "Wacky Wednesday" lunch menu, please use the spork and napkin icon at the bottom of the screen. Don't click the "Secret files" link. That will get you fired. After hitting "continue," I watched the screen divide itself into several colored sections, a "start here" link popping out of nowhere in particular, asking me to click it. Immediately, a list fell from a magical, invisible drop down.

You are attempting to leave to have a baby. As silly as that seems, we're here to walk you through the simple process of requesting leave. That is, if you really feel you must leave, and that our bathrooms aren't accommodating enough. We think it's a little rude, but, to each his own. It's not like we gave you this job right out of college. Like we were the only reason you were able to pay rent the month after you graduated. Your mother was so proud someone employed you, and now you're asking to leave. Great! We'll make it as simple as possible. Please follow instructions 1-10.

Maternity Leave Instructions:

1. Confirm that you are, in fact, pregnant and not simply out of vacation time. This can be discerned by how much gas you have on a daily basis and weather you're already on a written warning.

2. Know you have the option of giving us your first born in exchange for two extra paid weeks of vacation. Please see your supervisor.

3. Decide if being paid is really something you'd like while you're gone.

4. Find your HR representative and ask to fill out forms A through J.

5. If your HR representative can't find forms A-J, please complete forms K through Z.

6. Think about what this will do to your career.

7. Practice bending over.

8. Draw two vials of blood for reasons we can't disclose.

9. Assess whether you enjoyed the time you worked here. (Kidding, we know you're coming back. That's why we're making this so easy.)

10. Have your doctor sign all forms before submitting for approval.

I stopped bending over long enough to re-read the last line. No one had said anything about bringing my doctor into it, but protocol needed to be followed, and I was still stuck on blood-drawing—probably why I needed my doctor. The forms seemed to be the best place to start. Back went the email to Cindy.

Dear Cindy, may I please have forms A through J to fill out?

Reply: Paige

Dear Paige,

I found F through I. Hope that helps.

Cindy

Reply: Cindy

Dear Cindy,

That's about as helpful as a Band-Aid on a tummy tuck, but I'll take it.

Paige

A week later, I wandered into the doctor's office and peered at the nurse from behind a three-foot stack of papers. "Cindy sent me. I need the doctor to sign these so I don't have to have my babies next to the coffee kiosk in the break room. Even if they'd let me have some extra cup sleeves to lay on, I'm almost fifty-eight percent sure I don't want Caribou Coffee stamped on my child's butt cheek as he or she enters the world."

The nurse poked her hand through the stack of paper. "That'll be twenty-five dollars."

"For what?"

"Signing fees."

I plopped my papers on the counter. "I don't understand. How much does ink cost? Do you guys send out to have someone hand-grind it for you? I have a pen if you guys want to borrow it. It's a Bic. They're super reliable."

The nurse held up her hand.

"Now, just hold on, let me dig in this big old bag of mine, and get it for you. If it has crumbs on it, just brush them off. Oh, and the sticky stuff is just chocolate milk. I love chocolate milk for a hangover. Not that I've been drinking. That milk is from a long time ago. Don't worry."

"Ma'am, I don't think you understand. Any type of leave paperwork we sign, there's always a fee attached."

My elbows found the counter while I took a long look at the receptionist. A savvier person than I would've known that anything associated with doctor's offices comes with a hidden fee. As a child, when I broke my arm, the doctor tried to charge my mom for a "setting fee," a "removal fee," and a fee for any time I scratched at it without prior approval. She drew the line at a charge for any "unauthorized graffiti," told him to set it, and my arm still curves a little farther left than I'd prefer. I dislike this mostly because cyclists constantly think I'm waving them around.

This time, the doctors weren't getting off so easily. "If I pay your fee, what does it include? Hospital stay? No waiting in the cafeteria? I'm sure the massage after I give birth is included, but I want to know, in an itemized list, what this twenty-five dollars is going to get me. Oh, and you can still use my pen for that. I don't mind."

Her bouffant wiggled as she held out her hand. "It'll get you time off."

I handed her the papers. "Ok."

She smiled and signed the stack.

Triumphantly, I sent an email back to HR.

Dear Cindy,

My doctor signed all the paperwork. Please send someone to unshackle me from my cubicle when leave starts. I can't reach the chains over my belly.

Re: Paige

Dear Paige,

95

Thanks for getting the paperwork signed. Unfortunately, that needs to be faxed to our insurance company. If you can't fax it, you'll have to go on foot, but be sure and take someone with you. Safety in numbers and all that. The fax is 1-888-ancient-quest.

Cindy

Re: Cindy

Dear Cindy,

I really enjoy walking at this stage of my pregnancy. Thanks.

Paige

That night, I phoned the insurance company. "Hi, this is Paige Kellerman. I'm letting you know I'm sending in my paperwork for leave. I got it signed, and didn't drool on it, once."

"City and state."

"Excuse me?"

"Can I have your city, state, and reason for time off?"

"Phone person?"

"Yes?"

"It's on the paperwork I'm sending you."

"That's nice. City and state?"

"Phone person?"

"Yes?"

"I'm going to be faxing you forms F through I, tomorrow. I must hang up now so I can go find out how Danny

Tanner will deal with his daughter's high jinks before midnight. That, and there's a really big pie with my name on it sitting in the refrigerator."

"Ma'am?"

"Yes, phone person?"

"We'd be happy to approve your time off. What forms did you say you have signed?"

"Fantastic. I've got forms K through Z ready to go."

"Ma'am?"

"Yes, you helpful thing, you? Can I call you Adelaide? It sounds like what a helpful person would be called."

"Those forms are insufficient. We're actually going to need A through J."

"You are no longer Adelaide. That wouldn't be your name, even if it wanted to be your name. Which it's not."

After that exchange, I finished making my plans and sent one last email.

Letter to HR:

Dear Cindy,

I've decided to have the babies under your desk. Please make appropriate space by springtime.

P.S. If you ever find the right forms, go ahead and leave them out so I have something to rest my head on.

Paige

11
Piddle

Bladder control is one of life's greatest underrated achievements. Think about it. People are quick to point out someone's courage under fire, or another's perseverance in the face of adversity, but do we, as a public, thank the common man or woman for not peeing on things accidentally? I, for one, move that people not peeing themselves be acknowledged. It takes a lot of control for some of us, and a little pat on the back, or a complementary pack of Depends, would go a long way with the pregnancy set, both by wicking moisture and providing healing, emotionally. In the time since my pregnancy, have I gotten past lining my pants with plastic? No. But it'll take a while before I trust again. Great relationships need trust, and decent pelvic floor muscles.

Somewhere around the fourth month of pregnancy, an unknown individual forgot to put their bowling ball in the ball return and dropped it on my bladder instead, the pressure to relieve myself rivaled only by the pressure put on a grilled cheese sandwich in a George Foreman grill. Concerned parties innocently asked how I was doing, and found my mind completely engrossed in a urine-saturated state.

"Hey, Paige. How's the pregnancy treating you?"

"I have to pee."

"How far along are you?"

"Pee."

"Can I get you anything?"

"Peter Piper picked a pack of pickled peppers right before he had to pee."

"You want a pepper?"

"No, just like making obscure references to emphasize the fact I have to pee. Where's your bathroom?"

This sort of thing went on until the end of my pregnancy, and made everything from sleeping to going on dates with Husband nearly impossible. One Saturday night my love convinced me we should go out to dinner before we didn't have a chance to anymore. Agreeing, I pulled out the biggest duffle bag we owned, and loaded it with supplies. In went five extra rolls of toilet paper, some Depends, a change of underwear, a wet suit, and a laminated sign which read "Woman Peeing. Clearance: 50ft."

Of course, like any woman planning on spending several hours in a bathroom, an extra bag was in order for my reading material. Quickly, I tossed three Calvin and Hobbes collections, two newspapers, *The Beginner's Guide to Pottery*, and a copy of *Pride and Prejudice* into a plastic shopping bag. As I tied the handles over Elizabeth Bennet's face, I couldn't help feeling sorry for all the poor eighteenth-century women who hadn't had duffle bags or Depends. For that matter, when any of them were pregnant, how the hell did they even make it to the bathroom? "Forgive me, Mr. Bingley, but I must take a walk about the garden, for my bladder doth deceive me once again. Please join me so that you may lift my skirts high above my head." The sheer amount of fabric required to make a dress removes any doubt in my mind that that century must've been filled with women with dresses tucked into their underwear.

Dinner went smoothly, requiring a simple five trips to the bathroom before the entrees were served, another three after dessert, and an awkward explanation to a woman who'd knocked on my stall that I was only reading about pottery, not actually constructing an earthen bowl to give to the server for leftovers. I'd stuck my head under the door, stared her down, and said, "Honestly, ma'am, we take our dinner home in a paper bag like everyone else."

Frequent urination was annoying, but I was still the captain of my own ship. Urgency only interfered one other time, when our server stopped by with the check. "Can I get you anything else?"

My hand shot up. "Pee."

She smiled. "You wanted more steamed vegetables?"

"I gots to pee."

"We've got Pabst Blue Ribbon on tap."

I crossed my legs and my eyes at her. "Pee."

That night, we left with a to-go box filled to the brim with pie, peanuts, and three extra plates. The poor girl had tried to understand my bladder, bless her. I wrote her a thank you note when I got home.

Dear Heather,

Thank you for the pie. I peed right after I ate it.

Paige

One thing they don't tell pregnant women is how much better they'll relate to their grandmother after the whole thing's said and done. When I wasn't clenching my legs together in desperation, several occasions found me singing along to adult diaper commercials or dreaming about underwear made of plastic-cotton composite. If I went shopping for briefs, it was normal to stop at customer service and complain that "a layer is missing," and inquire if sending the mile-high briefs back to the factory was an option. Several times I was asked to leave, after I slammed my fist on the cash register and screamed, "Perhaps they could remember to put the plastic shell on, next time."

Park benches were the worst. If I noticed an elderly person sitting and feeding ducks, I always had the overwhelming urge to waddle over, sit down, and hold their hand. Looking deeply into their eyes and wrinkly soul, I'd whisper, "I know just how you feel. I just piddled a little on the bench, too." One man didn't take kindly to my encouragement.

"What are you talking about?"

"It's just, I know how it feels not to be able to trust your bladder anymore. I think we should rock back and forth in solidarity. Kind of like Hands Across America, but we have to call it something like Bladders Across the World."

He glared and scooted away. "I'm your husband and I'm only twenty-five."

"What about your old, wrinkly hands?" I asked.

"It's winter."

"You should use some of my cocoa butter. I'll get it for you, right after I pee."

Husband didn't understand. Men never do. Try telling a man you have to go to the bathroom for the fifth time in an hour, and he'll ask if "something's wrong." Never mind the fact the whole thing's his doing, and you reminded him you're pregnant, five seconds before. A man will always forget you're pregnant. "Why can't you go waterskiing?" "What's the deal with you not being able to run that marathon? You pull a hammy?" "Maybe if you tried a little harder, you could lift the Volvo so I can change the tire." It doesn't matter how many times you remind him you're pregnant, he'll keep overestimating your ability to do everything you used to. That's how I ended up in a movie theatre, clutching myself desperately.

Avatar. Lord have mercy if we didn't go see James Cameron's greatest masterpiece to date about people turning blue. Everyone else was. It was sketchy, but, from what I could tell, the plot involved half-naked Smurfs riding sea horses and making love to trees. But Husband championed the technology involved. "It's supposed to be amazing. Like, we won't even be able to tell it's animated."

"I can't go to the movies. I'll wet my pants."

"Why?"

"Remember when you thought we had a ghost in the house because you kept hearing the toilet flush all night?"

"Uh huh."

"Remember how I explained that you impregnated me so I have to urinate eighty times a night?"

"Yep."

"Ok, so, one more time. I'm pregnant, have to pee like a racehorse, and going to a theatre is terrifying. Even if it's to watch centaurs straddle pea-green goats, or whatever it is, in 3D."

"If you don't like James Cameron, you can just say so. I won't be offended."

"I like James Cameron. Actually, I think he'd understand what I'm trying to tell you. Only, he'd signal he understood by sending a terminator back to guide me to the nearest bathroom."

"So you're saying you've been wanting to see it?"

I hitched up my pants. "Sweet sassy molassey, let's just get going before I pee on something out of frustration."

Before we joined our friends inside the theatre, the frozen night air caused my bladder to clench temporarily while I watched Husband fork over a thousand dollars and grab tickets. Theatres are the enemy of pregnant women the world over. A seemingly innocent thing, houses which show moving pictures are actually as sinister as an expired carton of eggs, and terrifying for the same reason Siegfried and Roy's tiger hated being in that cage, went crazy, and developed a taste for sequined spandex: the illustrious cinema traps expectant mothers with promises of food and sedentary activity, and instead, exploits their weakness for being fed small treats.

To the casual observer, the movie theatre whispers promises of comfortable seats, unlimited snacks, and two hours of doing nothing but watch waifish actresses pretend they'll never ever get married because they own too many dresses, and end up falling in love with Channing Tatum after he's taken off his hideous glasses. And, as enticing as a thinly veiled plot of shakily concealed identities is, the casual observer couldn't be more wrong. Although, that spate of thinking did get the movie industry through the late nineties and well past the turn of the century.

What the theatre actually means for the impregnated is being dragged to a place where she's loaded up with salt, enough sugar to fill a cane field, and a drink the size of a Ford Windstar. The dear lady is then herded into a seat the size of a litter box and sealed in on both sides. Cruelty is what it is. My money's on the fact that if we were to examine every theatre seat in the world, we'd find at least three hundred expectant women turning in circles, abandoned and unable to find their way out, screaming, "Can someone take me to the bathroom? I think I just piddled on my Raisonettes." And husbands are more than happy to play into this insidious plan to make pregnant women urinate on delectable dehydrated fruit dipped in sumptuous chocolate.

It starts out innocently enough. "Honey, would you like something to drink? You look awfully thirsty. Let me buy you this gallon of Cherry Coke for being such a trooper."

She bats her eyes and accepts. "Gee, a cup as big as a station wagon? I'll have two. I just hope I don't have to go to the bathroom."

In my case, waddling into *Avatar*, a drum of Coke under each arm, was enough to set me up for a terror, once I laid eyes on the crowded auditorium. Like a bloated sheep, I was herded into the aisle, one boy shouting from his seat, "Mommy, I didn't know they let cows into the movies. How come that man gets to bring his pet and you made me leave the dog at home?"

Her response wafted over the aisle. "Honey, I don't know who taught that sweet dairy heifer to use a straw, but I don't want to hear one more word about the dog. A Shih Tzu would've gotten stuck to the floor."

It wasn't enough to be paraded around like a prize pig. Behind me, our friends, not necessarily sensitive to my condition, proceeded to strategically march my bladder and me to the middle of a chosen row of seats, seats positioned directly in front of the screen, sealed in on both sides of the aisle with no means of exit. Pregnancy message boards whisper it to be "The Land of No Escape or Hope." Or, as it's know to the French, "Territoire n'Appartenant à Personne." I prefer the French version, as it smacks so much less of desperation, peeing oneself, and the overwhelming urge to curl up and weep.

Under any other circumstance, finding a quick exit wouldn't have been a problem. I'd become a pro at figuring out how to bail in the middle of important situations to relieve myself. After all, I was four months in to the state of constant urination. I'd slipped out of more office meetings under false pretenses than MacGyver had perky mullet stylings. But, there in the theatre, there weren't any supervisors to convince I'd left my tights drying in the apartment oven so I could slip quietly down to a grey office stall. Glancing round at the solid blocks of people on both sides, my last hope was to figure out what an avatar was and beg it to hurtle eight rows of people, scoop me up, and spirit my rotund form to the bathroom.

As the gigantic screen began to fill with Gisele Bündchen–Smurf hybrids, beads of perspiration slipped down my forehead and plopped on my shirt.

Husband poked me in the arm. "Have some decency, woman. This isn't the time for a wet t-shirt competition, there are children in here."

"I don't think I can do this." The world was a desolate place, and I would both pee myself and die here.

"You don't have to wear the 3D glasses. You just won't be able to see the movie."

My legs crossed. "Not that, I'm gonna have to pee and I can't get out."

He patted my shoulder and handed me something in the dark. "Here, this'll help."

I felt around for a second. "What's this?"

"It's a popcorn tub. Just try to be quiet when you do your business."

"Thanks a lot."

"No problem. Now hush, the blue one that looks like Don Knotts is trying to teach the blue one that looks like that girl from *Center Stage* how to jump that sea horse."

Did I get my bladder under control enough to make it through the movie? Absolutely. I also figured out why movie theatre popcorn is so expensive. They have to scrub those tubs out really well afterwards.

12
A Note on Stretch Marks

Before getting married, I had a conversation with my mother about pregnancy and its effect on one's body. Let it be noted, this is the same woman who, while waiting to deliver baby number seven, had notoriously replied to my father's question of what childbirth felt like with, "Envision, if you will, someone jamming a railroad spike somewhere it's not welcome. You're truly missing out." Eventually the subject matter came to rest on stretch marks.

"Do you think I'll get any?" I asked.

My mom shrugged. "Well, they say it's genetic, so probably."

"And you still have a few?"

"Uh huh. Although, after the last baby, it just turned into one big mark, canceling itself out."

I continued filling in my eyebrows absentmindedly with a ballpoint pen. "Well, since you're stuck with them, do you ever find they're useful for anything? If I get them, I'm using them to hold change or bobby pins or something."

She considered. "I did get lost once, and, because the stretch mark on my hip looks somewhat like a map of the city, I was able to find my way to that Christmas party, on time."

I nodded. "Well, I've got years until I have a baby, so that'll give me lots of time to think of uses for my stretch marks. Who knows? Maybe I won't get them after all."

Mom smiled. "Maybe by that time we'll also be living on the moon, where gravity won't be pulling your rear down."

My hopes were dashed the morning I felt my first mark. I'd been looking for the other half of my Krispy Kreme doughnut when I found it lodged in a crevice under my stomach. And, being firmly entrenched in my second trimester, I hadn't been in any position to extract it. After one or two unsuccessful swipes, I yelled for Husband. "Honey, would you come in here? My breakfast's stuck."

A voice floated in from the living room. "Is it worse than the time you got that chicken salad sandwich stuck to your back and chased your tail until I got home from work? My rib hasn't healed yet."

"Possibly. Although, that chicken was in danger of spoiling. The doughnut may have a couple days." I batted at the pastry again.

Husband wandered in. "Well, where is it?"

"In my stretch mark. You'll have to fish it out. Speaking of, how bad does it look?"

He dipped down and regarded my stomach. "Kinda

looks like a crack I saw in the sidewalk yesterday. Does it hurt?"

"No, but I'm getting hungry."

Husband handed me the doughnut. "I'll leave you two alone."

For the rest of the week, I periodically rubbed my under-belly to feel the mark I couldn't see. It seemed to be growing, but I couldn't be sure. Finding hand mirrors useless, I utilized side view mirrors in parking lots and squatted over city fountains; both yielded a combined success rate of eighty-seven percent. Before long, I employed Husband's help once again. While he was watching TV, I waddled up and lifted my shirt over my head. "Look."

"Whoa, whoa, whoa. Easy there, Demi, this isn't *Striptease*. What's wrong?"

I eyed him while rubbing my stomach in circular motions. "I think they're growing."

His eyebrow went up as his eyes tried to navigate around me, but my belly had gone from formatted-to-fit-your-television to Panavision.

"What are growing? You didn't buy that deranged-looking Chia Pet on HSN, did you? Remember, if it sounds good after midnight, it's probably a terrible idea."

I waddled over and sat delicately on his lap until he tapped for air. "No, I think my stretch marks are growing." Going into free-fall, I sprawled on the couch. "Take a look."

Husband glanced down and regarded my stomach. "You sure you didn't fall asleep on the GPS?"

"Yes. Why?"

"It looks like a roadmap of Kansas down here." He delivered a poke to my belly button. "See, here's our house. Yep, the gutters need to be cleaned out. You know, we could charge people to see this. It's really pretty amazing."

Depression crept over me as I yanked my shirt down. "No, thank you. I suppose I'm just doomed to live life like a jigsaw puzzle."

He hugged me. "It'll be more like life as one of those chocolate crinkle cookies you see at Christmas. But I'll still love you and think you look great."

"You have to think that," I said. "You promised to love, honor, and keep me, all the days of your life. I'm not worried about you."

"Thanks?"

"It's just that my chances at the pool's Best Body in My Own Mind contest are looking pretty grim right about now. That blond with the black Toyota Sienna is gonna leave me in her perky wake of chlorine domination. The pool folk will simply refer to me as 'that lady with the lunch bag belly, who brings her kids to the pool in a rickshaw'."

Husband's eyes started working back around to the TV. "If you're so worried about it, I did hear from one of the guys at work that his wife uses this stuff called cocoa butter. He said she didn't get stretch marks." He looked at me from the corner of his eye.

"Well, how nice for her. Does she drive a Sienna with spotless leather interior?" But he'd planted a seed of hope.

What was this "Cocoa Butter?" More importantly, was it edible? The name suggested sensuality, but also hinted at being the main ingredient in a Paula Deen cookie. Maybe I used it to bake cookies, rolled in them, and then ate them until I passed out and didn't remember my body was betraying me. It seemed viable. At the rate I was being pulled apart, no one would want me after the babies arrived; my only hope for gainful employment would be as the understudy for Theater in the Park's *Phantom of the Opera*.

The potential of this new miracle cure-all fascinated me. If cocoa butter was, indeed, the answer, the internet would have a million positive responses, two million negative responses, and three million search results that had nothing to do with cocoa butter and everything to do with sloths named Cocoa who survived mainly by eating butter with the pads of their feet. I needed to get started. My chest was starting to look like two sandbags that'd been left out in the sun and kicked two times for good measure.

After talking to Husband, I'd plucked up the courage to wander to the bathroom and look directly into the face of my stretch marks, and what I'd seen hadn't been pretty. The canyons under my belly were invisible to me although I could feel them, but, if my thighs were any indication, an uprising was occurring. Seemingly bent on turning my legs into candy canes, red stripes wrapped around my ankles, doubled back, and shot up to my scalp. My boobs weren't much better. Little lines, forming due to the much needed creation of milk-holding hooterage, had turned my Bs into Fs. I was the proud owner of a new set of foobs. And those foobs had cracks in them a mile long.

When my Google search returned, pictures of skinny women seductively rubbing their stomachs bombarded the screen. The caption under a waifish redhead read, "I rub cocoa butter into my skin, once a day, and I haven't seen one stretch mark. Scientists think I may be a freak of nature, but that doesn't sell lotion, now does it? Try it and I know you'll like it. It may not help your face look as good as mine, but you'll likely retain the elasticity of two tortillas slapping each other." The whole thing sounded legit.

Before I continue, it's important to note here that cocoa butter can't be made at home. At least, when I tried to whack a coconut open with a butter knife, in order to spread the contents on my stomach, it didn't work out so well. There was lots of screaming and Husband shouting, "What the hell are you doing? Do you want to impale yourself? I'll go get a towel, just stay where you are." Then again, anyone savvy enough with Pinterest may be able to whip something up using old candle wax, glitter, and a cut-off sock. Pinterest didn't exist while I was pregnant, so I was subsequently forced to fail at crafts I saw in magazines and scrawled on the sides of rest stop bathrooms. But, I digress.

The next day, I sent Husband to the pharmacy to gather supplies. "I'll need a ten-pound tub of this cocoa butter, and not a drop less," I instructed from the couch. "If there are special gloves to rub it in with, grab a set of those, too. Latex is fine, but nothing stubbly like one of those weird bath mitts. Don't need to feel like I'm being groped by a majestic redwood. Oh, and a magazine, so I can read while I get beautiful. And a bag of M&Ms for Second Lunch. Hurry back, now. I may need your help to apply that stuff to all the spots I can't reach." I rubbed my hip absently. "There are some crevices I can feel, but can't see." Husband shuddered slightly as he closed the door behind him.

Some time later, after an extended period of time wondering whether a stretch mark could expand to the point it split open, spontaneously, and expose the inner organ which produces sarcasm, Husband came clomping through the door, strolled over, and slapped something into my outstretched palm. "Here."

I turned what looked like a giant tube of ChapStick over in my hand. "What is this?"

He shrugged. "Cocoa butter. Sorry, it's all I could find."

Taking the cap off, I poked at the solid contents. "You do realize I need about thirty more of these? We might as well use this to stop the bedside table from wobbling. It'll be like trying to spread a Tic Tac on a whale shark."

But Husband had already wandered off without a sound, leaving me to thoughtfully draw greasy cocoa butter circles on my face.

Refusing to be satisfied until I had a tub of something in my hands, I hoofed it back to the store in search of something more spreadable. Unfortunately, a quick scan of the shelves confirmed what Husband had already relayed; there were no gallon buckets of cocoa butter. Vitamin E, which had also been suggested by someone who worked with Husband, instead presented itself as a last resort. I grabbed a small tub, paired it with the cocoa butter stick, and thanked my lucky stars I finally had two miracle cures to put to work.

I might as well insert a quick "How To" when it comes to applying cocoa butter or any other lotion while impregnated. Because, as I discovered the hard way, misapplication can lead to over-greasing and the possibility of shooting through an open window.

You will need: a non-slip surface, your choice of stretch-mark-fighting lotion, a voice that carries, towels, a mirror, curtains over any windows you own, a ten-minute workout DVD of your choice, a hot shower, a pre-written contract for your husband to sign, jellybeans or another candy that won't get stuck in fat folds, a large spatula, and a three-hour nap prior to starting.

Step 1.) Although it's on the bottom of the list, napping before applying any stretch mark cream is a must. If possible, try to work in a full eight hours or take a vacation day so that an entire twenty-four-hour period can be dedicated to rest.

Step 2.) Post-hibernation, start the workout DVD. Get the blood flowing and the joints loose. I really enjoyed *Three Steps an Hour*, by Heins Slacker.

Step 3.) Hop…well, don't hop, but inch your form into the shower to get rid of all that sweat. Homeowners insurance doesn't cover "Whale Extraction" or "Accidental Shower Wedging."

Step 4.) Summon Husband to the bathroom to both help with shower exit and sign pre-written contract, which clearly states he will stay within shouting distance while cocoa butter is being applied. He is also not allowed to disclose anything he witnesses, no matter how horrific it may be. Try running through the "for better or worse" part of the vows, neatly outlining that this experience will clearly fall under the "worse" category.

Step 5.) Position yourself in front of a large mirror, and, after scooping up a large glob of cream with the spatula, begin slapping it on in even strokes. Kitchen Aid makes a really nice rubber spatula that's great for working around corners. Obviously, the back will be a hopeless endeavor, so this is where you can yell down the stairs, "Hey, I'm ready to be flipped," and waggle the spatula at your assistant.

Step 6.) Open the bag of candy to make the wait for your assistant more bearable. He will, no doubt, be dragging his feet up the stairs to make more time for throwing out compliments such as, "Why me?" "What did I ever do to deserve this?" and "I must be paying for that time I shoplifted when I was eight."

Step 7.) When he gets to the bathroom, wait for the screaming to stop before handing over the spatula. Explain that you can no longer see your inner thighs, and your back is a lost cause without him. Wait for the second wave of screaming to subside. (Please note: fanning your accomplice while whispering, "Shhh, it'll be over soon," may help.)

Step 8.) He's now in shock. Prop a towel under his head where he passed out next to the toilet.

Step 9.) When Husband comes to, place the spatula

in his hand and explain that your elasticity grew worse while he was out. And, if he could kindly resume with the dimple right above your butt, it would be greatly appreciated.

Step 10.) The lotion should now be fully applied. Before dressing, go lie down and wait for it to dry. Make sure to move cautiously, as any sudden movements may cause you to slide into the dresser, ricochet, and go flying out the bedroom window. Explaining away a flying, naked, pregnant woman is harder than it sounds.

I stayed enthusiastic about this routine for about a week. Then the excuses started.

Husband would stop me and ask, "Did you put on your cocoa butter today?"

"No."

"Why not?"

"I have to go mow the yard."

"Did you put on your cocoa butter?"

"Can't. I got invited to a very hush-hush dinner at the Royal Palace. They hate the smell of cocoa butter."

"Did you put on your cocoa butter?"

"I would've, but I got busy."

"With what?"

"Knitting."

"You don't knit."

"That's because we're talking when I could be pearling something into a sumptuous yet practical throw."

The truth of the matter is, applying cocoa butter, lotion, or Crisco during pregnancy is stressful and uncomfortable, so I simply avoided it after my first horrific attempt. Tempting fate? Absolutely, but I thought that maybe, just maybe, my skin didn't need the extra help. Perhaps angels would fly down as I slept and sprinkle magic Stretch-Be-Gone all over me, and I'd deliver both babies as unscathed as the very day I was born. Was it worth dying in a tragic "I oiled myself up and shot down the stairs, through the flat screen" type incident? Certainly not. If I go before my time, I'd rather the general public not discover my naked body greased smoother than Vaseline on a hairless cat, frozen helplessly in a state of reaching for the bowl of Skittles on the coffee table.

But the day of reckoning did eventually come. Shortly after bringing home my bundles of joy, I crept to the bathroom and surveyed the stretch mark situation I'd so carefully avoided taking care of. Where my belly button had once lived, a grumpy bulldog now glared back up at me, and from the looks of it, he had something of an obesity problem. I prodded him with a pointer finger. "Bad dog."

Pink streaks drag raced down my foobs and met a girl waving a flag at the bottom of my thighs. A curly stretch mark on my hip spelled out "Welcome home, sassy," and another on my left butt cheek expanded to the words "You Are Here," with a map down to my ankle.

Several months later, I advised my mom of the post-baby-body status.

"It's okay. Like I told you, stretch marks are genetic."

I set my stomach on the table. "Yeah, I put cocoa butter on, every day, so it must be genetic."

She smiled. "Did you really?"

I shook my head. "No, but at least now I have several places to carry change. Speaking of, can you break a ten for me?"

Note to the reader: during the writing of this story, all my stretch marks were consulted for accuracy. Any similarities to stretch marks of your own are purely coincidental. Also, if you're in the market for a half-used stick of cocoa butter, please inbox me. No stretch marks were healed in the making of this book.

13
Anything You Can Do...I Probably Can't

As I've mentioned before, men have a particular talent for not noticing when women are pregnant. I don't mean overlooking the almighty shelf we carry around, complete with book ends, souvenirs, and an old copy of *Southern Living*. No, it's much worse than that. It's more that the bump is noted, yet completely ignored, the sensory deprivation of a man prompting him to look past his wife's swollen ankles, hunched form, and intentional rhythmic breathing just in time to ask her to push the car while he tries to floor it out of a ditch.

Jump on any pregnancy discussion board and you're bound to see an entire section filled with comments from women whose husbands just "asked me to jump start the car," "couldn't understand why I didn't bend over to set the bear traps while he kept a look out," or "insisted it was my turn to shovel the driveway." One woman in particular reevaluated her relationship after she found out her husband had signed them both up for a marathon on her due date, and didn't understand why she "couldn't just run to the hospital," since it was on the route.

As the days of my pregnancy were riddled with such occurrences, I felt for these women. By the time the babies were born, Husband had earned his Doctorate in "Completely Forgetting Your Wife's Pregnant," making him qualified to ask questions like the following.

"Hey, some of the guys are going out for drinks and bungee jumping. Wanna go?"

"I can't."

"Why?"

"I'm pregnant."

"Oh. Is that a 'no,' or should I tell them we'll be late?"

Or, "You know, I heard they were offering couples judo down at the community center. Wanna sign up?"

"No, I'm pregnant."

"Well, you're the one who's always saying we need to do more things together. That's what I get for trying."

And, "Horseback riding?"

"No."

"Tandem bicycling?"

"No."

"You may have to look for a swimsuit that fits, but everyone's going water skiing this weekend."

"No."

Being reminded that one is excluded from most activities which entail fun is hard. Who doesn't love fun, besides the IRS? It's simply not possible to get excited about participating in anything while pregnant, especially pastimes that require movement, breathing, or smiling while breathing. Unfortunately, there are degrees of forgetfulness men tend to indulge in.

Like a shiv to the spine delivered in a darkened prison cell, the next level of ignoring a woman's pregnancy tends to be hardest on her back, psyche, and ability to fight the urge to smother her lover in his sleep with a one-hundred-percent down, Eddie Bauer, white cotton slipcase-covered, embossing-with-an-initial-is-extra pillow. Ladies and gentlemen, I present, for your pleasure, surpassing the "Why Can't You?" syndrome by sheer volume of audacity is the "Sure You Can" delirium.

Eighty percent of men with pregnant wives are affected by "Sure You Can;" the other twenty percent were, sadly, smothered in their sleep nine months ago. A newspaper article I read last week confirmed that they will not be missed, as their names were stricken from the record, the only initials marking their place on this mortal coil being "SYC."

Sure You Can Syndrome: noun: *A potentially fatal disease carried by men, which causes the afflicted to assume their pregnant wife can assist them in household activities such as changing a flat tire, stringing Christmas lights on third-story windows, and acting as a "brace" while finishing touches are put on the new wooden deck. Subject can be easily identified by the shoe usually found sticking out of his butt.*

I'm sad to inform you Husband was also stricken by this horrible condition. Before I was married, I remember seeing a pretty, blond, pregnant woman assisting her husband on an HGTV episode of *Look, We're Remodeling Something That's Different than the Other Stuff We've already*

Remodeled: Extreme Make It Better than Yours Edition. Her husband, ignoring her whale status, insisted she scale the cabinets, like an expert in guerilla warfare. En route, her water broke and ruined the new grout. The reality TV producers swooped in, adjusted the subtitles, gave the spiky-haired contractor some scrubs, and I enjoyed an hour-long episode of *Birthing and Loving Every Minute of It.* I won't lie and say my favorite part wasn't when the poor woman screamed, "I hated that grout color anyway!" and popped the baby out.

Although the backsplash tutorial had been top notch, I couldn't believe the nerve of such a man existed. Husband could never be that man. He wouldn't be. But then, we'd never had babies together before.

A blissful first trimester gone, an inkling of change began towards the second trimester. Husband started asking me for small requests. Could I hold this nail still while he hit it into the wall? The furnace needed to be replaced. Would I mind popping another one in? If I didn't have any objections, changing the oil in the cars was really a two-man job, but since he had to nap, would I mind scooting under there? Every time I saw him slink out of the shadows with a level in his hand, I and my watermelon would waddle the other way. After several such requests, it took him two weeks of looking to figure out I'd dragged the TV behind me, moved to the shed, and wasn't coming out.

"Don't you want to live with me anymore?" he asked through the clapboard.

"No, I like it in here with the spiders. They don't ask me to do ridiculous things that require a person to be concave, when I'm in such a clear state of being convex. And I don't care what you say, there's no way I could've fit behind the water heater, even with all that pan spray." In the end, he lured me back into the house, cajoling a fat lady with a trail of cake crumbs and the smell of a whole ham in the oven. Nothing gets me like a honey glaze.

Even with the promises of food and the seeming admission that I was, in fact, too fat to re-shingle anything, Husband's chronic SYC returned. Only this time, it was so horrible, I shudder to think of it. That's the thing about SYC; it comes and it goes. With Husband, its return was marked by a faraway look, an inability to hold still, and eight hundred feet of cable in his right hand. By the way he circled and kept poking me in the shoulder, whispering, "You'll do," I knew I was silently being nominated for something I really wasn't going to want to do.

"What are you doing with all that cable? Please tell me you've taken up free-form electronic basket weaving."

He continued circling and grunting. "Nope, I'm going to wire it."

"Wire what?"

"The house."

"Whose house?"

He grinned. "This one, but I need an assistant. I promise it won't be any trouble."

I backed away. "Males as thin as you are say it won't be any trouble, but that didn't stop me from getting wedged under the sink. And it still leaks. If you're so bent on wiring the house, why don't you tackle this one?"

His arms wrapped as far around me as they'd go, his

fingers resting on my hips. "You just have to look and make sure the cable's coming through the wall when I send it down through the attic. Easy peasy."

A quick aside on the word "just." Whenever someone, especially a man, says "just," it usually entails a laundry list of things. If your husband ever sidles up to you with his eyes wide, and starts throwing around the word "just," particularly in the context of "scurry up there" or "squat and hold it," please utilize the following statements to maneuver out of the room, before the situation turns direly out of your favor.

"I just don't think I can help you because our pet monkey hasn't been fed today. You know how he is about that. He's still irritate you named him General Peanuts."

"I can't. The non-alcoholic Jell-O shots are almost ready."

"My flat iron turned itself on again, and I smell my deodorant cooking. That whiff of juniper means I can't I help you, and possibly that a storm's coming."

"I can't. It took me eight days to summon Paul Revere's ghost, and this time it's going to work. I'll be in the basement."

"I don't mess around with my carpal tunnel. You know what they say about messing around with carpal tunnel. You don't? Well, one of us needs to look it up then. I return, post haste."

Run screaming to the neighbor's house is what I should've done, or at least used one of the handy off-the-cuffs just provided, but I didn't. My double chins and I silently squished together in a sort of fat kid nod of acceptance. I was too big, and had very little energy to object.

Husband grinned again. "You're the best."

I waddled up the stairs behind him. "The best what? Idiot you've ever met?"

Laughing, he led the way up to our bedroom, where a small hole had been thoughtfully pre-drilled a foot off the floor. He whipped around. "Here, take this."

"What is it?"

"An unbent coat hanger."

"And suddenly we're rich enough to waste coat hangers. Who do I look like, Ivana Trump?"

Using all the strength he could muster, Husband positioned my round form on the floor next to the miniscule hole. I couldn't see myself, but dollars to doughnuts, any passing Buddhists would've tried to buy and set me on their mantle. "Ok, Ivana. When you see the cable come down inside the wall, stick the hook in, grab it, and pull it out. Got it?"

From the floor, I jabbed the hanger back at him. "You better get in that attic, quick. Otherwise, I'm rolling after you, and you won't like what happens when I catch you. I move much faster with my legs tucked underneath me." Rocking a little from side to side, I growled.

Like a flash, he was gone, and, minutes later, I could hear him knocking around under the rafters, shouting, "Okay, okay. Here it comes. You ready?"

My legs had already gone numb. "Ready," I shouted into the hole, a big, fat Alice looking for her rabbit.

"What?"

"I said, I'm ready."

"You better be ready because I'm sending it down."

"I'm ready. Just drop it down before I give birth by the heat vent. If that happens, these babies will never be able to regulate their own temperature."

"Why are you going on about the heater? We're working on the cable." With that, there was a slithering sound, as something dropped through the wall and thudded softly out of my hole-vision sight. "Did you get it?" he asked.

"Roger that. I think I see it." Slowly, I stuck the hook through the wall and began fishing around.

"Did you get it yet?"

I pressed my lips to the wall. "I'm tryyyyyying to get it. Foot soldier to home base, you're being a bossy cow."

"I don't care about what you were watching on Animal Planet. Do you see the cable? I'm wiggling it."

"Stop wiggling it."

"What?"

Propping myself with my left hand, I used my right hand to continue jabbing at the cable through the tiny hole, Captain Ahab's inept, fat sister. "I can't get it."

One misplaced, jerky jab, and I rolled backwards, landed on my haunches, and stared at the hole which had just become my arch enemy. The baby on my right side poked my rib in reproach as it tried to right itself through the uterus.

A voice floated down from the attic. "What was that? Are you okay? Did you fall asleep?" Work boots thudded down the hall and burst in on me recovering my balance. "I thought you said you already took a nap."

"For crying out loud, man. I'm as big as a bull elephant. Help me up!"

Remembering I was pregnant for a split second, Husband took my hand and pulled me to my feet. "Listen, honey. If you didn't want to help, you could've just said so. Here, I'll show you how to do it." His lithe frame squatted next to the hole and peered in. "See, the cable's just out of reach. I'll run back upstairs, drop it down a bit, and you grab it with the hook. Remember when I gave you the hook?"

I brandished the hanger and gritted my teeth. "Yes, Peter Pan. I remember. She's a beauty of a specimen. Where would I be without me trusty right hand?"

Husband rolled his eyes and marched out the door. "Be ready."

I leaned out after him. "You be ready to run back down here when these babies come marching out due to the dangerous dance I'm doing with gravity and squat thrusts."

Hitching up my belly, hook in hand, I squatted in front of the hole and waited for the second coming of the cable. I wasn't eager to continue our little foray into home improvement, via my position on the carpet. By nature, squatting is a pregnant woman's worst enemy. Once she moves her belly that close to the ground, an entire arsenal of problems can follow from that much weight being shoved towards the Earth. Cracked floors, ruined foundations, inadvertent black holes, all possible. I'd heard somewhere that Stephen Hawking was working on a connection between a breach of the space-time continuum and an ill-placed pregnant woman.

Still terrified I'd be stuck indefinitely, I heard a voice trail down, "Here it comes!"

Immediately, I stuck the hook in the hole and began fishing frantically. Time was of the essence. Had I just peed myself a little when I lurched forward? Victoria had a secret, all right; her underwear should be terrified of pregnant ladies who try to wear it past the second trimester.

Finally, as if by divine intervention, the hook caught the cable, allowing the cable to be pulled through the hole by a woman who looked like she'd murdered and eaten an entire village of watermelons. Satisfied, I leaned back on my haunches and stared at the length of cable and the source of the cramp paralyzing my right butt cheek.

Husband came clomping downstairs and burst through the doorway. "You got it?"

"I got it," I said, gesturing toward the cable. "Now, if you'll excuse me, I have to rub Icy Hot on my butt and find a package of cookies to eat. If the Oreos are open, so help you. I'll pull this cable out and come looking for a handsome man in size ten work boots." Taking a strong hold, I climbed Husband's pant leg to a standing position. "Good day to you, sir."

He held out his hand. "Wait, you can't go yet."

"Why not?"

Patting me on the head, he said, gently, "Now that we've got the cable routed, I've got this TV downstairs I need you to hold while I mount it to the wall."

14
Poke and Prod

For those of you who've never had the pleasure of complete public humiliation, I feel it's my civic duty to address the subject of prenatal checkups, if for no other reason than to gift myself horrifying flashbacks and ghost sensations of having my backside caressed by foreign breezes. Most people don't realize it, but a great many things lead up to being wrapped in a flimsy table cloth and perched like a lumpy oatmeal cookie on a wax paper–covered table. I wish it was as simple as walking in and paying someone to scrutinize one's entire body. I also wish I had a trained ferret willing to bring me buttered English muffins in bed, but, such is life. If you or someone you know is headed to a first prenatal interlude, there are a few things to keep in mind.

Before one even thinks of attending a doctor's appointment, carrying some sort of insurance is a must. If you don't have it, pretending like you do will, at the very least, get you by the guard and up to the lady at the check-in desk. Her hair will most likely be in a bun, and she'll gaze at your form, trying to decide how you ended up in your current state. She will not offer you buttered English muffins. While you dig your ring out of your enormous handbag so you can explain how you ended up in your current state, she'll begin firing questions at you. "Name?" "Car you drove to get here?" "How many pets do you have?" "Do you know who your doctor is?" "Did that doctor know you were coming, or are you trying to sneak in her office?" And, finally, "May I see your insurance card?"

In my case, the insurance card had become entangled with my wedding ring, and I was able to easily pull both of them out together. She looked them both over with satisfaction, and held my card up to the light. "Gotta make sure it's not counterfeit."

Praying she wouldn't see where I'd free-handed the ID number and laminated it myself, I took a deep breath and waited for my next set of instructions. In a moment, a clipboard was being poked at my nose. "Here, fill this out to the best of your knowledge."

"What is it?"

"This is a *number two* pencil and a health history form. You'll need to answer all the questions, in the time allotted. Don't look at your neighbor's answers or ask another pregnant woman for help. If you lie about anything on there, the doctor will know."

I took the pencil. "If I fail, can I retake it?"

"No."

"Will you guys still be able to deliver my babies?"

"You've got a fighting chance. After all, it is multiple choice. Just don't assume all answers are C. Another one of our patients did that and had to start her third trimester over again. Looked rough."

Finding a seat beside another confused-looking pregnant woman mumbling something about her estimated weight, my clipboard and I settled in. I nudged her. "Hey, you don't know the answer to number eight, do you?"

She laughed nervously and began to cry. "I'm still stuck on date of birth. How are we supposed to know any of this in our current state?"

I looked at the questionnaire. It was rather long and seemingly thorough. Too thorough. Beginning with the preliminary information, I worked from top to bottom.

Name: Paige Kellerman

Reason for visit: Pregnancy

Patting myself on the back for remembering my address and phone number, I worked my way towards the next section, "Medical History." Admittedly, it did seem a little complex. The sobs from the lady next to me shook my chair as she whispered, "Blood type", and stabbed her pencil into a nearby *Parenting for Parents* magazine.

The directions were pretty straight forward. "Please fill out all ovals next to any condition you've ever had or think you may ever have. Don't lie. We always know when you're lying."

And then it said, *I have had the following:*

Diabetes

Heart attack

Monkey Flu

I stopped. Was it important they know about the

Monkey Flu? I'd put those days far behind me. Checking "no," I continued. The next section was drug history.

I have:

Done drugs

Known someone who does drugs

Thought about doing drugs

Never done drugs, but secretly snort Pixy Stix to look cool

Thought about crack five times since I got here

Either way you answer this part of the questionnaire, they assume you have a lab and will proceed to test for meth, along with high blood sugar. As it turns out, the high blood sugar is what they're really looking for, but more about that later.

After I'd navigated through the first two sections without passing out from exhaustion, the end seemed, logically, to be near. Then again, it would be reasonable to assume a health quiz would pertain to one's own health. And, just as a false sense of security settled over me, my pencil tripped the light fantastic right into the seemingly innocent category of "Family History."

Before continuing, I stopped and poked the lady beside me, who was working away her mustache with the pencil's eraser. "We're the ones having the babies, correct?"

She kept her eyes trained on a page full of un-filled circles as she whispered, "I'm not having your baby."

"Hmm. Ma'am, do you know what year it is?"

"Nineteen oh eight."

Looking over, I saw there were cloud doodles where

she'd also gotten stuck on "Family History." Couldn't blame her. This particular part had me stumped. I stared back at my paper, trying to speculate what my family had to do with the whole thing. And, for a bright, shining moment, a seed of hope took root and started building little Lego-block thoughts that I wasn't in this by myself. That, when the babies needed to come out, I would be allowed to pick three to five family members to divide the pain amongst. Although I loved Husband, he'd have to take on the contractions. I'd count for him.

But what's really meant by "Family History" is something entirely more sinister. I apologize, as I only have a rudimentary knowledge of doctor speak, but, loosely translated, "Family History" means "Taking into consideration that your pregnant brain doesn't remember anything at all, please list your entire extended family's medical conundrums, dating back as far as your lineage can be traced. If you need time to contact a historian, please fill out the form for a time extension of two days. Thank you."

I believe this is the part of the form which generally drives the pregnant woman over the edge. In my case, I barely recalled whether or not I'd parked in a handicap parking space when I pulled in, let alone whether my great-uncle Melvin had bunions during World War II, the frequency of their flare-ups, and if he'd been left handed or ambidextrous. Did I also know whether Melvin eventually got over his distaste of milk? If he could write with both hands, why didn't he ever answer his mother's letters on time?

If that wasn't bad enough, I needed to know whether Husband's side of the family had bunions, or chronic heart palpitations, or greyness of the gallbladder. Word to the wise, next time you find yourself on a date, skip dessert and go straight for the history of rabies and dry scalp. Years later, the doctor won't care if you had the Boston cream pie, but she'll be livid if you can't recall whether your spouse's second cousin, who was an albatross, had mange.

"Kellerman, Paige?" As I happened to be both a Kellerman and a Paige, I took note of the urgent voice, quickly filled in the rest of the ovals, and hurried over to a nurse motioning for me to follow her. Later review would reveal that, in my haste, I'd ended up diagnosing Husband's entire side of the family with gout.

The nurse who fetched me was nice enough. They're always nice. It's easier to get a timid animal to do what it's supposed to by reeling it in with pleasantries and promises of free stickers. I really shouldn't have hurried. Don't hurry. The health questionnaire catches you off guard, but know that the second half of the visit is worse. Take your time. Fill out the ovals. Contemplate driving back home and eating until you pass out.

All bright pink scrubs and substantial countenance, the nurse grinned at me. "Paige? Go ahead and follow me this way." She motioned down the hall towards a scale. "I see that you're new here, but I can assure you of the utmost quality of care."

"That's good to hear. After that mid-term in the waiting room, I almost dropped this class."

And, just like that, she transformed into a ringmaster

for Barnum and Bailey. "Step right up and see the wild bull elephant from Borneo tip our iron scales." She pointed at the scale and back at me. "Up, up!"

"What?"

Magically, a baton and top hat materialized in her hand. "Gather round and watch her take off her shoes and bravely make the climb."

As I stared at the metal scale, colored lights flashed and tenting dropped from the ceiling. "Umm, Nancy, was it? Is this really necessary? Can't you just make an educated guess at how long it'll take me to break this thing? I give it five seconds. Tops. "

But it was too late. Heads out of doorways, the mob amassing to observe the newest office fodder began to gain momentum. Nancy urged me on with her cane. "There's a good girl. Now, just hop on up there."

"Do I get any peanuts?"

"No."

"Handful of oats?"

"Don't make me get the hose."

I bellowed at the crowd and slowly mounted the monstrosity, a terrible creature with numbers everyone could see, specially equipped with built-in creaking action.

I hugged myself. "Nancy, it's cold up here. I'm scared." But the crowd had already started pressing around us.

The nurse waived her top hat. "Guess the weight. Guess the weight and get something pretty to take home to your sweetheart! You, down in front. How'd you like this stuffed frog or a shiny, new penny?"

All around, voices shouted, "Two fifty!"

"Naw, Marlene, she's obviously three forty," a husky voice shouted from the back.

"You're both crazy. She couldn't be a pound under four hundred."

If you make it through this second part of the visit, hat's off to you. By the end of my first round with the scale, I'd developed the overwhelming urge to run away to the circus and marry a trained bear named Howard.

In a daze, I hopped off and thanked her. "Nancy, that was delightful. Will there be a second showing, or am I allowed to retire to my stall?"

She smiled. "If you'll just follow me, I'll get you ready to see the doctor."

"Ahh, let me pick the straw out of my tail, and I'll be right behind you. By the way, I lost my balance when you were messing with the scale. I believe that tickle on my left butt cheek means I fell on one of your nurses. A broken ankle's nothing to scoff at."

Performance weary, I waited for the third and final installment of the visit, which loomed before me. I could tell the denouement of my appointment was nigh, due to a scarcity of a will to argue. Oh yes, by the time you actually get to see the doctor, your large form is putty in everyone's hands. On the way to the exam room, and before the drop off, Nancy convinced me to recite the most important parts of "Charge of the Light Brigade" while peeing into a cup constructed primarily to hold a Jell-O shot. This step isn't so much an installment of your journey as it is a reenactment of the not-Academy-Award-nominated *Panic Room.*

When it comes to peeing in the cup, not thinking about it is key. Otherwise, you end up in a corner screaming, "Just leave us alone. It's bad enough I'm trapped in here with Kristen Stewart. Now, take the money and get out." Do your business, don't get fancy with the calligraphy on the "name" section, and shove that bad boy through the metal door. The first time I had a go at it, perfectly-spaced block letters ate up most of my time. Mostly because multiple requests for a ruler, whispered under the door, were denied.

"Ruler?"

Silence.

"Ruler?"

Silence.

"An old, used needle it is then."

Also, don't worry whether your urine gets lonely sitting behind the tiny door for too long. I have it on good authority that there's a gatekeeper on the other side, lying in wait for your sample. It's a deadly serious game of "Crouching Lab Tech, Peeing Dragon." I've often wondered what the person on the other side of the door looks like. Possibly someone along the lines of Bette Midler in *Beaches*, just waiting to grab the brimming, yellow plastic cup, hoist it in the air, and triumphantly sing out, "Peeeeeeeeee for meeeeee."

Unfortunately, peeing in a tea cup doesn't excuse you from the last part of the journey. As I disrobed and hoisted myself onto the wax paper covering the exam table, the thought occurred to me that, if I'd had a little more resolve, climbing desperately through the pee cup door could have been a possibility. But, as I'd never been decent at dreaming the impossible dream or working my buttered body through keyholes, the staff had missed a delightful chance to extract me, feet first, and keep my rotund form in their nightmares forever.

The room was ice cold as I kicked my heels in time to nothing but my extremely regular paranoia. Like most people, I'd attempted to read a magazine while I waited for my new doctor, but the choice between *Forbes* and *Better Homes and Gardens* hadn't been enticing. Fat, naked women have little use for pie charts or hanging trellises.

A quick knock and the door creaked open. "Paige?"

"Tis I. Fat and naked. Nice to meet you."

"Nice to meet you as well. It's okay to take the gown off your face. We generally recommend you wear it. You know, for next time."

Glancing back at her clipboard, she tapped it with a pen and beamed. "Says here you had an exam only a few months back. We don't have to check you until you're much farther along."

God bless the woman. There should be a special place in heaven reserved for OB/GYNs who say, "Oh, it can wait until next time. Feel free to cover your muffin top back up." Although others may not be as lucky as I was. I've heard stories from other expectant mothers who state they knew their doctor better, on the first day, than a postman knows a mailbox.

Possibly sensing my apprehension, she kept it short and to the point. After confirming my due date, favorite color, and preferred live band at delivery, she smiled and said, "I just need to know one more thing."

I could sense the finish line and my undergarments waiting for me. "Yes, Doctor? I promise I don't care if the band's acoustic or not. Although, if you could pull a few strings and get all three Hanson brothers, I wouldn't hold it against you. They're all busy having babies now though too, so I guess one of them is okay."

She shook her head. "No, not that. We need to talk about how your whole family has gout. I'll need to keep you for a few more hours of testing."

15
You Can't Wear a Pup Tent

When she opened the Rubbermaid tub, I couldn't help laughing hysterically. Eyeing my friend critically, I watched as she began unrolling a circus tent and laying it out on the kitchen table. After I'd finished wiping the tears from my eyes, I took a giant bite from the chocolate chip cookie clutched protectively in my right hand. Crumbs fell out of my mouth. "Umm, why are we looking at blankets? I thought you said you had some maternity clothes I could borrow?"

She gave me a sympathetic look and thrust a table cloth over her head. "This is it, sister."

"This is what?" I poked my cookie at her. "A tablecloth? I don't even use tablecloths. Come to think of it, I haven't even used a napkin since Thanksgiving of 2005. And that was only because my tongue couldn't reach the gravy on my elbow."

"These, my friend, are shorts." She waggled the mainsail in my face.

I stared back in disbelief. "Are not. Those are grain

silos."

"I know you don't believe me now, but somewhere in your pregnancy, you'll need these."

"First off, I don't know anything about growing grain."

"Who said anything about grain?"

"Secondly, I'll never get that big. I was impregnated by my husband, not a sasquatch."

She laughed and continued pulling things out of the tub. "Here's a dress I loved, a skirt, and some tops. Oh, and you'll probably need this."

I lifted my forehead off the table. "What? What now? Is there a tarp in there that magically converts into a cool pair of pregnancy gauchos?"

Hanging off her pointer finger was an Ace bandage the size of Kansas. "This, dear, is a nursing bra."

"That's a tug boat cover."

"You'll notice the convenient slits on the front where your lady parts can make an exit."

My cookie lost its flavor. "That, you can keep. As it turns out, my boobs have already lost any and all elasticity. My grand plan is to drag them across the floor to the babies' room, and hang them over the crib until I feel like I've caught something. I've decided to call it Lactational Fishing. Still waiting on those copyright forms though."

For the next twenty minutes, my friend tried convincing me that burlap potato sacks were underwear and drop clothes were dresses. The world as I knew it no longer made sense. It was all too much. Before getting pregnant, I'd been aware that, once I did get pregnant, expanding was a possibility. "Expanding" of course meaning I'd be a size or two bigger, and maybe toy with the idea of unbuttoning my pants at some point. My form would model only chic things with hand-drawn birds on them, pants made of the softest linen, and tank tops which would draw comments I'd have to respond to with, "Oh, why, it does look like I have a grapefruit taped under there, doesn't it?" No one had said anything about tarps.

After I left her house, I decided it wasn't really my fault. I'd been duped into thinking I'd be able to wear the same clothes I had in college. For the past few months, I'd watched a pregnant girl at the office power walk from her cubicle to the bathroom. All office surveys confirmed she hadn't gained any weight, but had successfully swallowed a large albatross, the real kicker being she accomplished her daily jaunts in heels.

Like a pregnant Lord of the Dance, she hoofed it up and back. Never stopping. Never draping her svelte form over the water fountain and begging for assistance. Her calves were like two pieces of iron on an old-timey steam train, pushing her ever closer to pregnancy perfection. Her stomach floated in front of her like a crystal ball, quietly speaking of her future in New York's next fashion week. Observing her daily routine, I felt positive pregnant women didn't gain weight. And also that I needed to start working on a parade-float wave that, when copied, did her justice and convinced the judges I could be a close second.

If my sense of timing was anything nearing accurate, she gave birth on Monday morning and was back to work on Monday evening, appearing just in time to display to the entire workforce that she'd shed any and all weight within the last twenty-four hours, a small plaque on her butt reading, "These jeans are a size two. Thank for asking." I can't be positive, but I think I overheard her saying something along the lines of, "Oh yes, the baby walked out, cut its own cord, and then drove me home from the hospital, where I was able to get right back in to my routine of yoga, Pilates, and Zumba. It is Monday after all."

Pregnancy would be simple.

I would be svelte.

I would be an old-timey steam train with fire blazing from my caboose.

Fortunately, I snapped back into reality about the same time my first zipper broke and left me blind on my right side. Like mists blowing past a unicorn on a foggy morning in a peaceful woodland forest, my thoughts cleared. And what had originally been the steadfast thought that the woman in my office was the utmost in pregnancy quickly turned to verified thoughts that train woman was a freak of nature. The fact Ripley's Believe It or Not didn't have her in a cage somewhere was nothing short of a call for public outrage.

As it turns out, most women, like me, lose the ability to fit into their "normal" pants after the first couple months of pregnancy. At the sixty-day mark, I remember looking down and seeing a giant chasm between both sides of my zipper. To my knowledge, society hasn't seen a bigger rift than that since the great Lindsay Lohan/Hilary Duff standoff of 2003. Horrified, I tried pulling the sides closed, which only resulted in frustration and a muffin top the Pillsbury Dough Boy would've prayed to meet at a speed dating party. I needed a plan, a crowbar, and two tons of Crisco.

The first thing I did to cope with the new load I'd be toting for nine months was resort to the time-honored tradition of the ponytail holder. An interesting fact, historians date the holding together of a pregnant woman's muffin top back to the Mona Lisa. After complaining she felt fat, da Vinci handed her a dried piece of sheep's intestine with which to secure the bottom of her corset, and proclaimed, "Madam, I shall now paint you from the chest up."

I've always been a fan of extremely uncomfortable clothing choices, so clasping my pants together with something designed to barely keep hair in place seemed right up my alley. After all, nothing says "I'm having the time of my life" like a one-eighth-inch piece of rubber holding back yards of body fat ready to crush anything in their path. For any of the newly pregnant, I lend only one note of caution to this method of pant closure. Make sure the ties you buy are fairly sturdy and haven't spent a century wrapped around a hair brush. One particular afternoon, while standing in an elevator, my hair tie went rogue, snapped off, and blinded the woman next to me. My fat rolled out, hit the lobby button, and, as I tried to rein it in, we spent an awkward ten minutes bouncing between ground level and the second floor.

What the pony tail holder successfully does, however, is make darn sure you won't have anything to hold back your hair when you need it. If I had a dollar for every pregnant woman I've seen who looks like Don King with semi-ill fitting pants, I could've bought myself a new package of hair ties by now.

Eventually, the hair tie method fails every pregnant woman. After I'd broken every single one I owned, I realized, with horror, it was time to move into maternity pants—stupid, paneled rejects made of sadness and dolphin tears. As this was my preconception of the things, I wasn't happy about this turn of events. From what I'd seen my friend pull out of that Rubbermaid tub, and strange things I'd seen when attending the circus as a child, I was sure that giant pants were not only unattractive, but drew the attention of trained bears so they wouldn't rip anyone's face off.

Dipping my toes in the area of pants with more give than the Salvation Army, I started with a pair of narrow-banded, elastic-waist pants. Bears wouldn't notice, and they weren't exactly hideous. On the upshot, the small, three-inch band makes a pregnant woman feel as though she's still a part of the normal world, a world that gets up, buttons its pants, and proclaims, "I'm not a rodeo clown, even though I might've considered playing one in *8 Seconds* because Matt Dillon used to be pretty good looking."

A sturdy make, the band on these starter pants usually fits comfortably under the growing belly and is completely hidden beneath whatever tablecloth is being used as a shirt (more on that later). The band lulls the impregnated into believing she will weather the storm in a comfortable, chic fashion, and nothing will get in her way. I used to be proud of my band. So proud that I often flashed it at the lunch table and snapped it at unsuspecting victims. Jim in accounting didn't even see it coming.

"En garde!"

"Go away, Paige."

The narrow band was comfortable, held my muffin top at bay, and lied to the world that I wore normal pants just like everyone else. Until they no longer cut the mustard.

My mustard officially stopped being cut around the time my circulation started to be. The first clue was the tightening around my abdomen, the second being the horrible ripping sound my pants made as I walked, and the third was me turning blue, rolling down the hallway, and hearing the rest of the employees shout, "She's turning violet. Someone get her to the juicing room." I don't particularly remember the juicing process, but I do remember moving onto the next rung of the Pregnancy Pants Ladder.

They say you haven't lived until you've worn your pants under your boobs. As I tugged those unsightly slacks out of the plastic storage tub I'd exiled to the corner of my bedroom where I kept workout clothes, my "I'll drink until you're Channing Tatum" button, and any hopes and dreams of being thin again, I'd never felt so alive. Husband walked in just as I unfolded a pair of jeans. "What do you have my tarp for?"

"These are my new pants."

"You can't wear a tarp in public."

"Yes, thank you. I need something that'll cover my belly." I pointed at my former midriff. "This thing is getting out of control."

"And the baby books said you should wear a tarp?"

In response, I laid the jeans down at one end of the room and slowly unrolled the yards of fabric out into the hall. Three hours and two buckets of sweat later, I was ready to slip my formidable thighs into what roughly resembled a deflated hot air balloon. With a whoosh, I whisked the fabric over knees, butt, and ended up somewhere near my ears.

Husband raised his eyebrows. "Wow. Those are some pants. You said they were pants before this whole unfurling the sail thing started, right?"

That's the rub. Full-fledged maternity pants aren't really pants. A close comparison confirms they're more like an iron lung which requires a firm sailor's knot under the chin.

As it turns out, the giant pants I thought were only good for frightening off bears were nothing to be afraid of. Not having my circulation cut off was pleasant. And I discovered that if pulled correctly, the top of the pants gathered in such a way that I didn't technically need a shirt, just a snazzy necklace to give the ensemble some personality. A necklace also detracted from any negative side effects a cold room had on my now-bra-less state of affairs. For any ladies who find themselves in this stage of the pants process, try dwelling on the benefits of trousers that hit you above the shoulder.

- Ready-made penguin costume.
- The ability to be your own sleeping bag.
- Storage for your Kindle and other assorted paperbacks. (Author's note: make sure to throw some Purell in your hobo bag, in case one of those

books heads a little south of the border before you're ready to read it. Stephen King's *Salem's Lot* is good. It's just not as good if it smells like butt.)

- A chic briefcase, until you sit down and crush the contract for that account you landed that was bigger than your pants.

- Finally, giant pants are a great conversation piece when the conversation lags at places such as the DMV: "Hey, you guys. This wait is long, but I bet you my pants are longer."

I used to flirt with Husband this way. If I ever wanted to fool around, I'd saunter over to the couch, tug at the pants string around my chin, and coo, "How long do you think it'll take to get these off me?"

To which, he'd reply, "I could be dead by then."

"You cad," I'd say, batting my eyelashes. "Just let me grab the scissors and we could have these off by sunrise."

The only thing that turned Husband on more than my pant-earmuffs was the assortment of tops I collected over the nine months. It started out innocently enough. For the first few months, I watched my regular shirts get smaller and smaller, my pub crawl t-shirts shredding and snapping at the seams, tank tops inching up until they hit me just below the nostrils. It wasn't until I was accused of indecent exposure at a McDonald's that buying bigger shirts even crossed my mind.

"No, ma'am," the manager said. "Unless you stop wearing that tank top as a bandana and cover yourself with something, we can't give you the three McFlurries and one straw you ordered. Even the fry cooks requested a day off and counseling services in order to fix the damage you've done here today."

I held up a hand. "You don't understand. This is a shirt."

"That, ma'am, is a blanket for a pygmy hamster, clinging to a barge. Pull through and leave."

I covered my chest with the car's operation manual. "You guys offer counseling?"

"Well, we give all our employees a free apple pie and a number to call."

"You're saying I can't have my McFlurry?"

He shook his head. "I'm saying the woman working the grill saw you and can't stop weeping uncontrollably."

"But—"

"Good day to you."

My course of action was clear cut, if horrific. To function in polite society, I needed to head back into the Rubbermaid tub and pull out that mainsail I'd seen hanging around the bottom. I didn't want to do it, but things were looking grim. Twice, the neighborhood watch had called me in for nearly exposed headlights, and a local gang had stopped me to find out where I'd gotten the bandana tied under my arms. The latter was awkward because being interviewed by a gang can be a lot of pressure. Was I associated with the south or east side chapter of Homicide Inc? Was I throwing the gang sign or having a contraction? Did going by the street name "Bubbles" sound okay, or would I like to keep my married name?

So it was with great reluctance that I snapped open the tub and let my first maternity shirt billow. Miles of fabric rolled over my palms and hit the floor with a thud. "Thar she blows, Cap'n. She be strong enough to get us to Tortuga and back."

Husband called from downstairs. "Everything okay up there? You knock something over?"

"Just my pride, sweetheart."

"Oh, ok, because it sounded more like you shot a deer with a crossbow and it hit the TV."

There was no doubting what I held in my hands was the largest shirt ever made. While I waited on the phone to speak to a representative from the Guinness Book of World Records, I examined the blue drapery panel I was now required to wear as a top. Strings jutted from every angle, and the waistband went on for days. There was a complete road map of Texas printed under one of the armpits, and under the other one, a tab that said, "Pull here to inflate in case of emergency water landing." For the next eight hours, I worked on putting it on. By the ninth, I wandered into the bathroom, looked in the mirror, and realized I'd mummified all my fat. Success.

Here's the thing. If the marketing departments of all major maternity retailers would just be honest with the general public, instead of creating cruel, cruel lies in the form of size-two women who look like they should be flailing around on the beach doing a print ad for Calvin Klein, most women would be prepared for the pup tents soon to be sported along with their bumps.

As it is, print ads and commercials for maternity clothes are something close to a conspiracy. Those catalogues have a lot of nerve. "Hi, my name is Becky and I'm adorable."

"Hi, Becky."

"Thanks for looking at our new spring collection. Unfortunately, you'll never look like this in a tankini because I started out a size zero, and you started out a lot bigger than that. Please expect to feel like an elephant when you order and don your new 'Fun-kini' in Floral Madness."

"But I always look great in anything Floral Madness."

"You won't this time because airbrushing out your hips isn't included. We don't even ship overseas, so…"

"Listen, Becky. Despite the print, I feel there's enough yardage here to do the job. Look, they've got my size in this box with the elephant overlay measuring its waist. Twelve feet by twenty feet. Perfect."

"True, there's more than enough material in stock. The only problem is your hips will roll around under there like two sailors in an arm wrestling match for who gets the last case of rum and goes down with the ship."

"I see."

"Please expect seven to ten days for shipping. Also, if you enjoyed our selection of shirts, please visit our underwear section. Because you should treat yourself to a good cry in your holey granny panties today."

After I fully embraced maternity shirts and got past the ridiculous advertising, there was no turning back. From church to grocery shopping, the fabric around my middle created a mainsail that made the boy sacking my groceries scream at the cashier, "Batten down the hatches!" and all the faithful at mass pray, "Dear Lord, if it be Thy will I be swept to my reckoning by the folds of that woman's relaxed-fit jean apron shirt, please make it quick and smell of Downy dryer sheets. Amen."

I could feel my blood circulating, the feeling coming back to my torso, and I finally had enough time to read by flashlight underneath my double extra large cotton t-shirt (those Choose Your Own Adventure stories are absolutely timeless). My spirit felt free and ran unfettered in pants that hit me at the shoulders. I was one with the Spandex. The Spandex was one with the frightening dips and curves of my enormity.

It was a comfort I hadn't known could exist while pregnant. The freedom made wandering to the old Rubbermaid tub a joy. Nay, something I looked forward to, the right side of my bottom lip bitten in anticipation. On any given day I might end up in a plum muumuu or be spirited away by a circus tent, black and romantic like two crows flying over a still lake at midnight. The pure romanticism and beauty of the thing assured my heart I'd probably never give that tub away. Mainly because I'd named it Hansel and given it its own space at the dinner table, but also because, even after my babies have grown up, I may want to drag it out, extract the biggest pair of cargo shorts the world's ever seen, and show my grandchildren exactly what they'll be inheriting when I pass on.

16
Stork Parking

I don't like to think there's anything like pregnancy SWAG (Stuff We All Gestate For), but there's a certain something an unknown, fantastic person thought up that's changed the way pregnant women park, forever. Rivaling only the toaster, "Expectant Parking" or "Stork Parking" may be the greatest innovation in the last century. Anyone who pipes up and vouches for the hoop skirt can exit quietly. The bigger I got, while impregnated, the harder it was to do physical things like run, lift, and pay taxes. And, while I was aware being pregnant came with small perks like being able to order pie, say you're going to eat the entire thing, and have nobody try to stop you, Stork Parking was a way to finally say, "I'm here. My water hasn't broken. And I'm out of bread."

Yes, pregnant women have now been lumped in with others who need a little more help to the door, and I'm not complaining. By the time the end of the third trimester rolls around, it's all you can do not to hire someone to pull your massive form in a decently sized Radio Flyer whenever you need to make it from the Ford Tempo to the inside of the gas station in order to purchase one more Slim Jims. I know. I tried. Unfortunately, there's a serious shortage in the amount of available people who are willing to pull a two-hundred-pound woman around in a child's toy for little to no money or a coupon for twenty percent off at Bed Bath & Beyond. So it was with great joy that I embraced maternity parking when I first came across it.

But, as with anything that may be a perk in life, before I could take advantage of it, I had to season it liberally with a healthy dose of guilt and apprehension, guilt exacerbated by Husband the first time we thought about using one of those Holy Grails of parking.

A routine trip to Best Buy found us scouting the parking situation. The anxiety as we went round and round the occupied spaces was overwhelming. What if there'd been a massive rush for Mariah Carey's *Greatest Hits* and I went home empty handed? Did I have enough candy left to soothe that kind of pain? Realizing that heading back to our garage, parking, and then walking back to the store was our only option, we'd all but abandoned the idea of going in. That is, until I saw the "Maternity Parking" sign.

"Ohhh, we should take it. It's made for people like me."

Husband surveyed the empty spot right next to the door. "You mean people who don't shower regularly?"

But my head was already out the window. "No, this says we can park here because you and I did the Tango of Love and expedited the process of me getting fatter than a housecat who found the Little Debbie stash."

"But you're not that big yet. What if people think we're lying?"

I hadn't thought about that. What if I didn't qualify? My bump wasn't totally visible yet. If anyone started asking questions, the best I could do would be to point to my first trimester muffin top and plead impregnation and not Chunky Monkey. Surely they didn't make you pee on a stick in the parking lot. That seemed both costly and awkward. Could we get a ticket if they didn't think I qualified? And, if we went to challenge it in court, would the judge simply look down and pull out a picture of the pregnant woman who'd really needed the parking space and had keeled over because she'd had to park at the Chipotle and was now hospitalized from exhaustion and a bean-induced charley horse?

The sad fact of the matter is I'm rather lazy. Pregnancy combined with laziness prompts one to tell her husband he worries too much, and to park the car before he's forced to let her ride piggyback while slapping him with her wallet and yelling, "Onward, Sea Biscuit."

I was able to avoid turning myself into an unusually large jockey, and we made our way into the store without anyone asking us how we had the gall to steal rock star parking from women whose waters were breaking in the washer/dryer section. The Mariah Carey CDs had been saved by a barricade of Nickelback albums. And all was right with the world. Although, it seems I vaguely remember hearing a woman's voice from the plasma TV display huskily wheeze something about the long walk from the car and how, if she wasn't going into labor, she'd nudge the baby's head back in and take this seventy-inch flat screen home right now.

Unfortunately, the seed of doubt never quite removed itself from the rest of my pregnancy. Whenever I saw a maternity parking spot, my fatness came into question. I'd been bold at Best Buy, but would it fly at the grocery store? Doughnut shop? Sally's Half-Priced Muumuus 'N' Things? For the remaining trimesters, any time I spotted a "Stork" parking spot, I circled it like a pregnant hawk, debating with myself and gauging the circumference of my belly. If it was a go and there weren't too many people watching, I'd commit and cruise into the rectangle capped with the picture of a stoned stork holding an infant in a questionable-looking handkerchief.

Collar pulled up, enormous, dark, Nicole Richie wanna-be sunglasses in place, when I finally gained the courage to shut off the car and struggle out the door, I did my best to thrust out my stomach to quell any questions of authenticity. Because there was judgment. Oh yes, judgment around every corner of my mind. I knew everyone was staring at me, measuring my belly with their eyes. On particularly paranoid days, I'd take off my coat, tuck my shirt into my underwear to accent all my curves, and start massaging my middle all the way into the store. If anyone looked my way, I'd start moaning things about Braxton Hicks and how I hoped my water didn't break again in the bread isle. What produce stocker really wants to deliver a baby, I lamented loudly.

But, as Audrey Hepburn had made abundantly clear, the charade will eventually suck you in. Also, Cary Grant by any other name is always charming. I started feeling entitled. It's the other side of the tiger, as the old saying I made up goes. Though I'm not sure of the tiger's symbolism or which side is better. However, what's clear is, if you give a pregnant woman a regular perk, she'll start believing she's always had it. This is mainly because nine months is long enough to convince the average woman that she's always been pregnant and always will be. After about the sixth month of being pregnant, I usually answered the question, "When are you due?" with, "Due? Due where? I canceled my interpretive rhythmic gymnastics ages ago." The pregnancy would never end, and neither would my sweet, sweet parking spot that bested even elderly parking.

I was a pregnant American. And as such, there needed to be a stork stalwartly holding my spot no matter where I went. If there wasn't a spot with my name stenciled in the asphalt, someone out there hated me. How did they expect one such as myself to drag my enormous ham hock of a back end all the way from the cart corral to the produce section? Even Husband started to notice if our reserved parking was missing, pointing out that a certain local supercenter demanded we park thirty feet away, like commoners.

"Don't they know you're pregnant?" He looked at me like a confused fox caught in a bear trap.

I shook my head furiously. "You'd think so, right?"

"Maybe we should go to customer service and explain the situation."

I nodded. "Good plan. They probably don't know

how babies are made. Which is so weird because I know I saw an entire stack of *What To Expect When You're Expecting* on one of those huge…" I flailed my arms.

"Displays?" He rubbed my shoulders.

I set down the paper bag I'd been breathing into. "Yes! A de-splay, that's it. So they must know. And since we had to park with all these plebeians, it means this particular supercenter hates me, hates pregnant women." My eyes narrowed. "Wants us to exercise."

"That's terrible." He used a page from the car manual to wipe the tears from the corners of my eyes. "They probably don't know you break out in hives if you move faster than a snail in a salt mine."

"I know, but let's go in anyway. That thirty-pound bag of Charleston Chews isn't gonna buy itself."

It took me a long time to realize I wouldn't always have my own parking spot. Even after the babies arrived, I parked wherever I wanted. It wasn't until the parish wrote me a very to-the – point, but kind, letter explaining that I wasn't to park next to the nativity scene that I reconsidered what I was entitled to. Besides, it was getting pretty tough to reverse out of the pew, all the way down the aisle, and out the door without hitting people I was sure God liked a lot better than me, people who walked from their parking spaces and didn't take out the entire ceramic sheep population under the tires of their SUVs.

Three years and thousands of ceramic sheep later, I've finally made peace with parking amidst the regular people. But that doesn't mean that when I come to your house I won't be parking in your living room. Because we all forget sometimes, and if you really like me, you won't say anything, and just chalk it up to me being thirty-six months' pregnant.

17
You've Got the Diabetes

Somewhere around my twenty-fifth week of pregnancy, the doctor sat me down and handed over a little bottle of orange liquid.

I grabbed at it greedily. "Ooh, what's this? No one said there'd be bonus Kool-Aid for making it to the next round. But I'll take it. Could I trouble you for a straw? And some crackers. I love Kool-Aid with some nice, crispy Wheat Thins."

She shook her head and pulled a piece of paper from a cabinet above her head. "Next week, I need you to come in, drink this, and then we'll make sure you don't have diabetes."

My heels tapped the exam table. "Impossible, I haven't been bitten by a raccoon in ages." I did a mental review. "Or ever. That may have been an angry neighbor."

She shook her head. "No, this will help us tell if your blood sugar is alright."

"Husband always tells me I'm sweet, so that's a good sign, right?"

"Not exactly."

"Yeah, I don't believe him either. Because, after that, he's always like, 'Hey, will you hand me the remote? I can't reach it.'"

The piece of paper she handed me spelled out strict instructions for taking the test. No studying involved, but, apparently, I was required to drink the orange stuff, not eat before the drawing of the blood, and the results would confirm whether I had diabetes or not.

"So, what happens if I have it?" I rolled the orange bottle around in my hand, still contemplating sticking a straw in it and asking for another.

"You'll have to go on a diet, test your blood sugar every day, and stay off sugary foods for the rest of the pregnancy."

The room started spinning. I put my hand up. "Did you say no more sugar? As in, I wouldn't be allowed to make little towers out of marshmallows on my belly, knock them down, and eat them one by one, singing the various character-assessing songs from *Willy Wonka and the Chocolate Factory*? As in, 'Oompa Loompa do-ba-dee doo, I'll eat another marshmallow or two.'" My breath escaped in gasps while I clawed absently at the wax paper under me. "No more late night Oreos or early morning trips to Sonic for Route 44 cherry limeades?"

"I'm afraid not."

"The same diabetes that Wilford Brimley is always going on about but makes me think about oatmeal, instead? And then I get all confused and forget it's not a commercial for oatmeal and find myself in the kitchen trying to heat up that last instant package of Apples & Cinnamon stuck to the side of the cabinet with old honey and even older diet aspirations?"

She inclined her head. "Yes."

The world suddenly seemed a foreign place. "Listen, Doctor, I don't think you understand. My plan was to prop these atrocious-looking ankles up on the couch and hire someone to bring me chocolate milkshakes until these babies started wandering towards the light."

But she was gone, and in her place was a card telling me when to come back and face uncertain depression. Because every pregnant woman loves to be confined to the edge of her seat, right where's she's most likely to fall off or break it in half.

Weeks passed, and the next appointment finally moseyed its way around. At the same time that my date with the needle reared its ugly head, I did something bad. Not clubbing a baby seal bad, but along the lines of noncompliance. As in, "I'm Kurt Russell, and I'll escape from New York my own way." The nurse found out first.

"So, what time did you drink the Glucola?"

"Was it orange, kind of bubbly, looked like the melted Popsicle no one wanted?"

"Yep."

I shook my head. "Then I have no idea what you're talking about."

She looked concerned. "It's imperative you take that test as soon as possible."

"No, 'imperative' is how I feel about urinating these days." I felt my cheeks getting hot with the effort of trying to stay in the right, when I so clearly was not. "So, if I drink that stuff, it'll just end up coming out of me, and then we've come full circle. What does that make us? Full circlers, that's what. Good day madam."

And with that, I grabbed a new orange drink and waddled out. They were on to me. What was so bad about high blood sugar anyway? Determined to find out, I turned once again to Google and confided my private, only-the-thousands-of-people-who-work-at-Google-can-see-it query, and waited to see how justified I was in skipping my test.

As it turned out, I was perfectly justified. For instance, if I skipped another test and went undiagnosed, I could only end up with massive health problems, type two diabetes in the future, and a baby that grew so big, we'd have to hire David Copperfield to coax it out using the ancient art of sleight of hand and salad tongs. Considering this information carefully, I decided to take the test, and I passed.

Wait, no I didn't. Sometimes my memory likes to rearrange itself to make looking back a more pleasurable experience.

The devastation was dealt swiftly, over the phone. "Hello, Mrs. Kellerman?"

"Yes?"

"This is Nancy from the doctor's office. I'm sorry to inform you, but you failed your glucose test and will need to come in for another appointment so we can teach you about the diet and the equipment."

I set down the giant doughnut I was making love to

and brushed the crumbs off my "I love sugar. Just ask me about it" t-shirt. "Failed? Pardon me, but I haven't failed anything since that biology test in college, and who in their right mind knows how warm a tree frog needs to be before it wants to mate? Apparently, 'when it puts its socks on' wasn't the right answer, but to be honest, I don't think my professor had ever really asked a frog."

Computer keys clacked over the line. "How does the day after tomorrow sound? I can put you down for a two o'clock with the nurse practitioner."

"That sounds fine. I'll just be giving this doughnut a nice funeral in the trashcan. Oh, and Nancy?"

"Yes?"

"What was that about equipment? It doesn't sound all bad. I've been looking for an excuse to buy that Gazelle thing I keep seeing at three in the morning. Not that I want thighs like Tony Little, but that man brings a sense of majesty to the fine art of galloping in place."

"You can pick everything up at the pharmacy. We've already phoned it in for you."

"Sounds great, Nancy. And I think it's fantastic they can order workout equipment so fast."

"Goodbye, Mrs. Kellerman."

Two days later, I picked up my mystery bag of supplies, shook it once for luck, and headed to the doctor's office, where I pulled up a seat next to the nurse practitioner. Shaking my head, I dumped everything out on the counter. "Ok, there are quite a few things in here, but nothing close to a Gazelle."

"A what?" Her pen scratched diabetic things down.

"A Gazelle. You know, like on the thing. Doesn't matter, I'm sure it's being shipped to my house."

She motioned to the brown bag holding the supplies. "Ok, Paige, if you bear with me for a moment, I'll show you how to draw your blood and test your sugar levels."

"Listen, Gertrude, was it? I don't have time to play games like 'Shank Me Once, Shame on You.' I just need someone to show me how to bring these levels down, and I'll take it from there. I've come to terms with saying goodbye to sweets. Although, I can't swear I won't sleepwalk a gallon of ice cream into my mouth. Everyone knows sleepwalkers have no idea what they're doing. And even though I've never sleepwalked, there's a first time for everything. In fact, I could go to sleep right now and probably wander to a Sonic or something. I've been served, like, eight cheese coneys there, in my pajamas."

Ignoring my pleas, and harnessing the swiftness of an American bald eagle on meth, she opened boxes, shoved a needle in a small harpoon gun, and handed it to me. "You get to try it first. Don't be nervous. You just pull the little trigger, listen for the click, and you'll get enough blood to put into the glucose meter. Pretty simple."

Horrified, I pointed the harpoon back at her. "No, simple is what Betty Crocker has worked lovingly into her brownie recipes for the last fifty years. This is what civilized people call barbarous. Let's play a fun game called 'You Stab Yourself First,' Gerty, and then maybe I'll follow suit if I happen to lose my mind in the next five seconds or so."

But the lady who looked like she may have been a

Viking milkmaid in another life insisted, and waited patiently for me to maim myself. She nodded toward my pointer finger. "Go ahead."

"I can't."

"You can."

"Generally, when someone says they can't do something, it means they're unable to at this time. Or possibly ever. Only time will tell. What's the old saying? 'If the young bird is ready to fly, push her out of the nest, unless she has diabetes.'"

Patiently she waited for me to pick a finger to impale, while I stared back at her like a Kodiak who'd just been asked to shove its foot into the bear trap to make sure the spring was set right. Slowly, I looked down at all five fingers on my left hand. Which one did I like the least? My thumb was out; I needed that to give double thumbs up when I did something cool and no one was there to validate it. I occasionally had to pick my nose with my pointer finger. I never had to flip anyone off with my left hand, so that was a possibility. My ring finger was out. Stab it anymore, and my wedding rings were never going back on. My pinky looked so unsuspecting, I couldn't bear the thought of surprising it so much that it might fall off. Silently, I set my sights on the left middle finger and cocked what might as well have been a Colt 45.

Gerty smiled. "Go ahead."

Squeezing my eyes closed, butt cheeks tensed to maximum capacity, I pulled the trigger. There was a soft click, the sensation of being slapped by the world's smallest monkey, and then the tiniest amount of blood. Sighing,

I dropped the blood on the test strip and shook my head at the nurse practitioner. "Geez, Gerty. With the way you were building the whole thing up, I thought it'd be horrible, but that wasn't so bad. You shouldn't scare people like that. I was all, 'This won't be so bad,' and you were all, 'This is going to be the worst thing you'll ever do in your life.'"

She popped the test strip in the meter and watched the numbers flip past. "Right now, your number looks a little low. I'll go through what you should be eating and at what times."

I stopped wrapping my finger in the scrap of cloth I'd torn from my dress and put down the tongue depressors I'd gotten ready to form into a make-shift splint. "Oh, I can help with that. I usually eat all day, breaking for five minutes in between each meal, and then a midnight snack at midnight, one am, two am, three am, and six am. After which, I have breakfast."

The milkmaid gave me a sad look and continued. "You'll need to have three regular meals and three snacks. Here's a portion guide and a list of foods you're allowed to eat."

The list wasn't long, mainly because it was missing most of the major food groups. "Where's the bottom of the pyramid?"

"What pyramid?"

"The food pyramid." I stared at the sizeable nurse practitioner blankly. "You're a medical professional. You know the one I'm talking about. It goes meats, cheeses, dairy in spades, and on the bottom, good food like Little Debbies and oatmeal cookies. That's why grains are on the bottom too. Well, wait, wait, I guess it's more of a plate shape now, so all the sugar would go around the outside, with a little sprinkled on each portion."

She shook her head. "No sugar, sweetie. Sorry."

"I thought you guys were joking about that part. As in, 'Oh, when we said sugar we meant you'll have to lay off using the stairs and other assorted physical activities.'"

"That's actually not what we meant at all."

"Are you sure? Because I could definitely lay off physical activity. Except for that Gazelle I'm still waiting for. I totally thought the doctor was kidding. She's such a kidder, with her ability to kid and such. Really, no sugar?"

Cheerfully, she spent the next twenty minutes elaborating on the goodness of wheat, the saintliness of vegetables, and the joys of soy enemas. Ok, I may have imagined the last one, but she might as well have, for all the fun I was having. (Please note: I'm not endorsing a soy enema in any way, shape, or form. Unless you're one of those organic people. In which case, as you were.)

"But, as you can see, sugar-free foods are okay in moderation."

I stopped planning a slow walk in front of a quick bus long enough to catch the last of my kamikaze food instructions. "What was that?"

She nodded. "Sugar-free desserts are okay in small servings. That means you can have sugar-free ice cream, pie, that sort of thing."

For a moment, Gerty disappeared and the angel Gabriel appeared in her place, carrying the biggest fruit cobbler I'd ever seen. Beams of light radiated around the large, wooden spoon he held out to me. There was hope. "So, my good Gerty, that would mean sugar-free candy, cookies, and cheesecake are all on the table?"

"In moderation."

"Moderation. I'll have to look that up sometime. Say, isn't that when you can't poop?"

"That's constipation."

"Right." I tapped the tiny harpoon gun to my temple. A whole new world had just opened up to me. There was a way to beat the system of no desserts, and its name was Sugar-free. "Gerty," I said, "throw those needles in a bag. I've got a date with the grocery store."

18
A Note on Sugar-Free Crap

I've always been a fan of things that taste good. In fact, as far back as I can remember, the tendency to gravitate towards food that's awesome has been strong within me. Kind of like the Force, only it gives me incredible gas instead of the ability to move things with my mind. So it's hard to imagine why anyone would try and make food horrible. It's true I ruin food on a regular basis, but never on purpose. The difference between broiling and boiling is something many people have trouble muddling through. Regardless, there are those who invent horrendous food and attempt to play it off like it's delicious and tastes just like heaven in a pan. I speak, of course, about sugar-free food, poop's second cousin.

Of course some people, like diabetics, can only have sugar-free things. And after the devastating diagnosis of gestational diabetes by my doctor, I suddenly found myself staring at new and limited food choices. Being the inexperienced idiot I was, my hopes were pretty high for sugar-free foods. Unfortunately, while my doctor was scrawling down "weight—two billion pounds" on my chart, no one bothered to sit me down, look me straight in the eye, and say, "Paige, you can have sugar-free desserts, but please know that 'sugar-free' roughly translates to 'Food that has lost favor with God.' When you eat it, your mouth shall turn to sand, and all your dreams will wither like a grape in the sun, or under-eye circles in a tanning bed, or your confidence when you told that boy in high school you liked him and he rebuffed you while stocking yogurt in the dairy case."

The thing about me is, I'm an optimist when I'm taking a break from being a pessimist. And even though "sugar-free" didn't sound that great when the milkmaid nurse practitioner suggested it to me, I also knew food makers made things like ice cream, candy, and pie from the stuff, so it couldn't be all bad. Gathering what I remembered from almost minoring in history, that's also what the Trojans said right before they wheeled that giant, oak stallion through the door.

"Captain, it's a giant horse."

"How big?"

"As big as a Carnival cruise ship."

"There a tag on it?"

"No."

"Seems legit. Wheel it in."

Never mind. I bet the Trojans wished that thing had been filled with tasteless, sugar-free cobbler instead of death. But I digress.

Inexperienced, hungry, naïve. As I marched down the frozen food aisle and towards the ice cream, I couldn't help feeling I was beating the diabetes a little bit. I wouldn't be sad and grow a moustache like Wilford Diabetus Brimley, or eat oatmeal until my bowels sagged. I'd march right down to those foggy doors, rip them open, and proclaim, "Revenge. Aisle eight." And, for a moment, what awaited me was beautiful.

It was obvious; sugar-free people knew how to turn me on faster than Josh Hartnett handing out samples of free sunscreen and offers of a mole mapping. I fell to my knees and wept, my arms wrapped around the ankles of a passing stock boy, the cuffs of his corduroys clenched in my fists. "Have you ever seen anything so beautiful... er...Dylan?"

He shook his leg a little. "Do you need help finding anything, ma'am?"

I ran my hands over a frosty row of sundae cones. "Dylan, if tomorrow never comes, just know that I'd like to be buried here, amongst the sherbet. Please tell my husband, as he may not be aware of my new plans. For he loves sherbet, and may wish to lie next to me."

While Dylan ran off to tell the store manager they needed to call the police on a diabetic cougar, I stood and gazed lovingly at all the selections the freezer case had to offer: ice cream sandwiches, fudge pops, chocolate penguins holding little electronic glucose meters, and, of course, the aforementioned sundae cones. Grabbing eight or ten boxes, I loaded up on my sugar-free booty and headed to the candy aisle, where delights almost as equal waited for me. The selection wasn't as grand, but I wasn't going to haggle over why there weren't sugar-free Skittles or M&Ms instead of questionable sugar-free red hots.

In fact, most of the sugar-free candy looked like it belonged in a senior citizen's crystal swan bowl, but I happened to be the type of person who didn't mind swans, got along great with senior citizens, and was looking forward to tricking my mind into thinking I'd had sugar. Bags of candy-shaped items sporting the tags "Sugar free!", "Same Great Taste!", and "You'll Never Know This Isn't Licorice!" tumbled into my cart by the arm full. They made fantastic riding partners with my sugarless cookies, sodas, and dental floss. I paid for all of it. Went home. And then one of life's harshest truths was revealed to me—the four lies about sugar-free food.

For those of you who've never had the pleasure, the four lies are as follows: It's good. It tastes just like the real thing. You'll forget you just ate sugar-free food and think it was real food. You'll be happy after you eat it.

Sugar-free ice cream, also known as "Yogurt's Ugly Cousin" or "Spackle," encompasses all four cardinal lies. Sure it's cold, it's creamy, and it usually comes with a colorful label that looks like the colorful label on any other ice cream container. There may even be a cow on it, or an innocent-looking hippie with a spoon. The only problem is, what's waiting on the inside doesn't taste like ice cream. If you'd like to recreate the consistency and experience at home, walk over to the refrigerator, stick your hand in the freezer for thirty seconds, remove it, and then lick. No need to wash the hand before trying. You want it to be as authentic as possible.

I gave some of this delightful dairy confection to Husband. Mouth clenched, fists balled, and only after forcing down the abomination he had in his mouth, he looked at me and said, "Woman, are you trying to kill me?"

"What?" I flicked the dandruff off my sweater, innocently. "You don't like it?"

His shaking hands grabbed my shoulders. "Is it because of what I got you for your birthday last year?"

"I don't remember what you got me for my birthday last year."

"Obviously you didn't like it. Otherwise you wouldn't be trying to kill me." Delicately, he pulled the blanket from the end of the couch over his head and curled up in the fetal position. "Don't bother me for a little bit. I need time to knit my insides back together."

I forced down another bite. "Oh, it's not that bad. This is the only type of dessert I'm allowed to have until the babies get here."

His eyes widened over the edge of the blanket. "You're only allowed to eat ice flavored with plaster? That can't be good for the children. They'll both come out looking like little, chalky cherubs."

I shrugged. "Then we shall put them in the garden, and wow the neighbors with our elegance. Possibly attract butterflies. Possibly get HGTV out here to recognize the undeniable need for help with our foliage situation. It's getting out of control."

For the remainder of the pregnancy, Husband put large crosses on all of the sugarless food, and spent every Sunday dowsing them in holy water to keep evil spirits from leaking onto his *Double Double Double Strawberry* ice cream complete with extra sugar, infused with packets of sugar, rolled in braised sugar. Every time the freezer opened, all I heard from the kitchen was, "It's still here. You keep back. Honey, is there any more holy water left?"

The rest of it wasn't that great either. Sugar-free candy is about as much fun to eat as the "shift" key on your keyboard. I'm convinced diabetics and the elderly look serious most of the time, not because they're angry, but because, if they don't use every ounce of concentration, that imitation Werther's is going to fight its way back up an esophagus and make life very difficult. The tragedy being, of course, that this experience is the opposite of relaxing on a sunny porch swing doused by the sweet rays of twilight, as shocks of wheat blow delicately in the wind, reminding the eater that life doesn't get better than communing with nature, licking caramel and holding your grandpa's hand. Nope, candy devoid of sugar is more like licking that porch swing, and getting excited when the splinters don't get lodged in your tonsils.

Husband also swore off sugar-free candy, giving it points only for looking like real candy, and extra points for its ability to make him question his faith in the entirety of mankind.

And yet, I kept eating both the ice cream and the candy.

One day, while using a sugar-free chocolate to seal off a cracked pipe under the sink, Husband looked up at me. "How do you eat this stuff?"

I considered. "Have you tried it when you're unconscious?" Painstakingly, I continued sanding the cabinets with a caramel.

Although I wouldn't wish it on any of you sweet people reading this book, if any of you find yourselves stuck on the Good Ship Sugarless anytime soon, and realize you need a little help ingesting either ice cream, candy, or something tastier, like sugar-free pie, try one of the following suggestions.

Eat it while you're in a coma.

Eat it after you've fallen down the stairs, and you can't taste it past the pain of the ankle bone sticking out of your flesh.

Eat it after you've passed on to the next world. I hear everything tastes better in heaven.

Eat it while being chased by a panther. You probably won't even notice the weird taste it leaves in the back of your mouth, as this can easily be confused with the bile you're throwing up due to the sheer terror of the situation.

The fact of the matter is, when you're addicted to sugar, as I am, you'll try anything just to get a hint of the former glory. For weeks I shoveled down sugarless ice cream, candy, soda, broken dreams. To make matters worse, I'd been placed on a diet so strict that I started receiving letters from Vegans of America telling me to "live a little." All the lean meat, graham crackers, and "fresh vegetables," whatever those were, did their best to drive me back to the sugar-free desserts, repeating the four lies, and convincing me things without sugar would be an oasis in the desert.

"Paige," they'd whisper, "eat that nasty lettuce and you can reward yourself with a delicious scoop of sugar-free strawberry ice cream. It'll taste great. No, better than great. At the very least, it'll wash the taste of salad with no dressing off your palate. You won't even notice that the strawberry-ish aftertaste in your mouth will be something akin to eating fried couch cushion. But they won't be run-of-the-mill cushions. They'll be nice ones, like something you can't afford from the Land's End outdoor collection."

After a while, I'd completely forgotten what real desserts tasted like. It'd gotten so bad that, a few weeks postpartum, when a waiter brought me a slice of legitimate French silk pie, I slapped him with my starched white glove and started screaming things about how decent pies taste like contact paper, Mod Podge, and failed attempts to get into community college.

It took several months post-partum for me to accept the fact that I could have real sugar again and that the sensation of eating dessert was supposed to be a pleasant one. The doctor cleared me, but I'd been brainwashed into a healthy lifestyle.

One Sunday, Husband sat me down and spelled out "good" in my palm with chocolate pudding. "Take it slow," he said. "It'll all come back to you. It's just gonna take some time and chocolate milkshakes at regular intervals."

It was all smooth sailing after that. My taste buds grew back. I learned to trust ice cream again, and I have a new-found respect for anyone who has to manage diabetes on a full time basis. But to this day, I look over my shoulder, making sure the Viking milkmaid nurse practitioner isn't watching me make love to that Snickers at midnight.

19
As the Belly Turns

I suppose this is as good a time as any to mention something about the dangers of having a large belly. Twins or no, when one gets impregnated, the resulting stomach expansion carries with it a host of hazards besides flattening the occasional toddler or inadvertently knocking out your best friend's German shepherd. On the upshot, toddlers are, at least, smart enough to duck. Unfortunately, German shepherds won't respond to warnings in German, unless they were actually raised in Germany. But I didn't know that, and Wilhelm will be greatly missed. At any rate, there were a few things no one bothered to mention to me about belly maneuvering. Otherwise, Husband wouldn't have been parked behind the steering wheel, staring at me like he had when he'd found out I like to eat Oreos in bed every night and spread the crumbs into a sleep-able surface.

"Umm, are you okay?"

I stopped flailing my arms long enough to consider. "Okay" was such a relative word. Hotel pillows were "okay." Having half my paycheck taken by the government was "okay." Owning a flat iron that did the job but slightly singed my ends off a little more each time was "okay." Being wedged between the car door and the garage wall fell somewhere between "okay" and "I may just quit this thing called Life." I sucked in the available air supply and tried to wriggle free again. "Hold on. I'm just gonna suck the baby back towards my spine and try this again."

Husband knit his brow. "Are you sure? Because you really look stuck."

"That's nonsense. People don't get stuck in their own car doors."

He turned the key in the ignition. "You're stuck. Just let me reverse out and you can climb in after I've cleared the garage."

I shook a fist at the air in protest. "But I'm already half in. It'll feel like failing." Breath shot out my nose. "Not to mention, I could get even more jammed than I already am. There's an excellent possibility my spine either just broke in half and shot into my right butt cheek, or the weed whacker fell off the wall and you're going to have to come extract it."

"That sounds terrifying."

"Yes, but remember, you promised to stick around for better or worse. Even if I'm about to give myself a lawn equipment enema."

It'd all happened so fast. I'd been innocently waddling down the garage steps, playing "Which Board is Most Likely to Give Out," when, the next thing I knew, a routine hoisting of my massive form into the little, white four-door became a situation best handled by the Jaws of Life.

I suppose I should've seen it coming. Day by day, fitting behind the steering wheel had become a chore. I didn't even have to use my hands to turn it anymore. Utilizing almost-non-existent abs, I simply gyrated a little bit and the vehicle lurched in the general direction my belly button was pointing. Parking was the only time I actually had to pay attention, and then all I had to do was incline my chest and glide into the first maternity spot I found. Either that, or make it to the grass, occasionally leaning my head out the window and shouting, "Ladies and gentlemen, we're coming in for a landing. Please return your tray tables to an upright position and thank you for flying Large Bellied Airways. Ground control, please verify that it's safe to land and that parking on this Ford Taurus is okay. Over and out."

Unfortunately, fitting behind my steering wheel wasn't the only problem. By my eighth month of pregnancy, the belly had grown to such substantial circumference that I needed to walk sideways through elevator doors and airplane hangars. Calling ahead to grocery stores so they could reserve two bag boys ready to hold the automatic doors was a must. Too many a time those sliding, modern marvels had gotten impatient and tried to close on me while I squeezed through and desperately attempted to anchor myself to a cart.

Others had begun to notice the gigantic size of my belly. At work, one of my coworkers tapped me on the shoulder. "I just told that guy over there you're having twins. He said that was a huge relief."

I leaned my belly against the cubicle wall. "Why's that? I mean, obviously more people who look like me on this earth is a good thing and will breathe new life into the eHarmony dating sites of tomorrow, but was he particularly worried about it?"

She laughed nervously and looked around. "No. He thought you were only having one baby and looked way too big for that. No one told him you were expecting two. So, yeah."

I let out a sigh. "Well, I'm relieved that he's relieved. I wouldn't want anyone losing sleep over my circumference. I'd just feel awful if I knew he was over there experiencing sympathy contractions while trying to decide why one baby was causing me not to be able to fit through the lunch room doors. Seeing a lady in the hallway eating and trying not to get run over by the janitor is rough. Yep, my heart would be totally broken if I knew him to be in such turmoil."

She looked around again and laughed. "Yeah, so I gotta go."

I didn't wander over to talk to the man in question myself. Because, as much as I wanted to coddle and tell him not to weep over the potential labor or surgery I was about to have, I had other things to worry about—like how I was going to get someone to carry me down two flights of steps. Three times that week I'd jammed the elevator doors, and maintenance had informed me they were "getting fed up with calling the fire department to have the doors forced open and everyone carried out."

Ridiculous co-workers and broken-down elevator

aside, the other all-important thought consuming my mind, while stuck between car and garage, was figuring out how to circumvent my belly and shave my legs, so the surgical staff delivering my babies didn't think they were helping birth the only other sasquatch known to man.

Yes, while Husband's main concern was how he was going to un-jam his wife from between the garage wall and his car, she was mulling other things over, like all the places her razor was missing every time she stepped into the shower. No one talks about that part of it, about the things the big belly politely tells you you're going to have to work around. *What To Expect* may have mentioned something about growing as large as a circus tent filled with elephants, but I don't remember anything about needing to learn yoga just to shave a decent bikini line, or my legs, or my tarantula belly button. When you can shave only what you can see, it's a good idea to name your nether regions "Wild Kingdom" and commit them as a wilderness preserve for endangered pheasants.

When it came to taming my werewolf legs, getting in the shower wasn't the problem; for that I had a couple of options. Trial and error had led me to construct a complex Rube Goldberg–like contraption that ran purely on dominoes and duct tape, the purpose of which was to launch me over the side of the tub and deposit my rotund form within biting reach of the loofa. If my invention failed, I'd have Husband play a nice game of Hot or Cold to coax me into the right spot.

"Am I getting close?" I'd yell at the doorway.

"Getting hotter. Just a little farther forward. Yep, there you go. You're standing in the tub."

"I am?"

"Can't you feel it? I figured the dirt on the bottom would be the tell."

"I just can't see anything past this stomach. I figured I was either in the tub or stepping in the toilet again."

A door opened downstairs. "Good luck with that."

Once I made it into the tub, I had to trust that my feet were where I'd last seen them nine months ago. Looking down, all I saw was what appeared to be the backside of a great albino whale getting ready to dive for plankton. Carefully, I stacked what I needed on top of it: shampoo, conditioner, razor, body wash, shower radio, loofa, whistle in case I fell out, laminated copy of US magazine, and some sugar-free snacks sealed in small plastic bags, just in case I got stranded for a few days.

Shampooing and conditioning my hair and washing my face usually went smoothly. Even the task of wielding a loofa around my massive form didn't present any particular dangers. Although, I harbored an unspoken fear of accidentally losing the fluffy washcloth hybrid in some sort of unmentionable place where even spelunking couldn't retrieve it without a crack team on the case. It wasn't until my trembling hand pulled out the razor that all my joints seized up in terror.

Now, a lot of women I know quit shaving after their stomachs got too large during pregnancy. But I wasn't some woman; I was Paige, distant cousin to sasquatches everywhere, missing link of the shower set, and I refused to let my bottom half grow as wild as the Garden of Eden without so much as a pruning.

The thought of having the babies, losing the weight, and realizing I looked like a faun from the waist down was too much, even if it did help me get a part in the city's fall production of *The Lion, The Witch and The Wardrobe*. Besides that, I knew, during a C-section, there was a fantastic chance everyone and their mother would be able to have a gander at what I had going on under my backless hospital sundress. I refused to be held singularly responsible for half the medical staff quitting, and the other half questioning their beliefs in science entirely. The conversation potentially bouncing around my nether regions echoed in my thoughts.

"Dr. Smith, I thought you said we were doing a C-section today. This creature looks like it needs a good shave and rabies shot."

"You know, Dr. McCoy, I think I saw this species on the last episode of *MonsterQuest*. I believe proper protocol dictates we quarantine it and call the Discovery Channel."

"Nurse, get my cell, a razor, and a Sudoku puzzle. We could be here awhile."

"Right away, Doctor."

The mere suggestion that an entire team of people would be looking at me unclothed was motivation enough to brace my hand against the shower wall, grasp the razor with my other hand, and begin poking around in a land where nothing could be seen but only felt. As my hand passed beyond the belly point, I waved goodbye and wondered if what it was heading towards was an ankle. I knew there were two of them down there. And if I kicked just right, both ankles became visible, wrestling around in the bottom of the tub like two competing boars during mating season. As I chased each swollen cankle with the Bic, I could hear squealing. Sometimes I made contact and snagged a hair; other times I drew first blood and waited for them to retaliate by whipping up over my head and slamming me out onto the bathmat.

With each attempt at this terrifying routine, the sad fact of the matter became apparent that everything beneath the belly line had become invisible. And as frustrating as realizing that my legs were slowly becoming a preserve for mites and other small, hair-dwelling creatures was, nothing compared to the knowledge that my lady region was also out of control.

I told Husband the news one day while sadly motioning towards my sacred space. "You're just going to have to get used to it."

"You mean you can't shave it by Spider Sense?"

"Darling," I said, smiling, "you tell me how comfortable poking at your crotch with a paring knife while blindfolded is, and I may reconsider it. But you'll have to be willing to go first. Afterwards, the damage will be assessed, and I'll let you know whether I'll be following suit. Until then, we'll just pretend this is nineteen oh four."

So, back in the garage, as my hairy self was still pinned between car and garage wall, I waited patiently while Husband backed out and released me. Because even if the neighbors were feverishly snapping pictures of the evening when that Kellerman woman almost got squashed to death, I took heart in the fact that, although they, too, now knew how many problems my belly was causing me, none of them could see the wild forest I was concealing from the world, my doctors, and the Discovery Channel.

20
Get Thee to a Birthing Room

My maternity leave request had been approved after going through human resources, the president of the company, three janitors, and one very nice man from the FBI who said that a few questions were standard procedure. I said goodbye to co-workers, cleaned the snacks from my desk, and prepared to waddle off into two, full weeks of vacation before I replicated, twice.

Pooling my vacation time and a couple loop holes into the leave process, I'd managed to finagle extra time off, time I'd be spending on all the important last-minute nesting things my brain told me needed doing before I gave birth: cleaning the oven, organizing the utensil drawer, and finishing arranging the magnets on the refrigerator. All things the babies would be checking for when they got home.

I was geared up to eat takeout, watch re-runs of *Charles In Charge*, and practice—on Husband—all the ways I'd learned in birthing class to de-gas a baby. He never responded well to being swaddled, but I felt fairly confident he'd be okay with me peddling his legs and mixing the smallest amount of soy into his beer.

Two days into vacation, I'd been able to check "eat five times a day" and "sweat profusely on my way to the bathroom" off my To-Do list. Swelling had set in to such an extent that when my sister dropped by for a surprise visit, she asked how we'd had enough money to hire a bouncer for the front door, and whether she could get by to see the lady of the house. She looked me up and down. "You're huge."

I rubbed my giant ankles together. "Thanks, I think."

"No, really, I think you might have preeclampsia."

We stood in silence, listening to my calves expand. I scratched my hip. "The doctor didn't say anything about excessive hair growth, but, now that you mention it, I kind of feel like I'm wearing a pair of fur tights. Then again, my razor and I aren't really seeing each other right now."

She shook her head. "Preeclampsia's when you have excessive swelling, and is actually pretty dangerous."

I waived her off. "Well, I'm going to see my doctor tomorrow, so I'm sure she'll let me know if I've got pretentions."

"Preeclampsia."

"Right."

I put any worries about preeclampsia out of my mind, until I found out the next day that I had it. Three days into vacation, not so much as an organized utensil checked off my list, and I had my mother knocking on the door.

"Hi, Mom. What's up?"

She looked me up and down. "Your doctor's been trying to get a hold of you."

"She called you?"

She marched in the door. "Yes."

"Why didn't they just call me? Wait, you're not pregnant are you? This would be a fine time to steal my thunder."

She sighed. "They tried to call you but your phone's—"

"Dead. Right, I forgot."

"I thought you were dead."

"I'm not."

"She called me because I'm your emergency contact. After they saw you this morning, they ran tests and decided your preeclampsia's too bad to wait on. They want you to head to the hospital."

I leaned towards the stairs and cupped my hands. "Honeydew? Get your Sunday best on and water the horses. We've got some birthin' to do."

Husband walked down the stairs. "What? Now?"

Smiling, I motioned towards my mother. "Yep. Apparently, I can stay home if I want to, but I might go into shock or something. How good are you at slamming someone's heart back to life with your fist? I never asked you before we got married. That, or your thoughts on the burgeoning deer population. What do you think? Hunt them, or let them flourish like a herd of wild, untamed, beautiful butterflies with antlers?"

But there was no answer, just the sounds of my bag being thrown in the car, the engine revving, and one man preparing to be a father. If you're wondering what that sounds like, imagine two elk in a power walking competition.

So much for my full two weeks of vacation before the blessed event occurred. Organizing the remotes by size and taking a Magic Eraser to the car bumpers would just have to wait. I grabbed a snack, bid adieu to my mom, and waddled towards my destiny. Oh, and drugs. I waddled towards lots and lots of drugs.

21
The Blessed Event—It's Raining Drugs

Someone once told me the key to a great birthing experience is never taking your eyes off your opponent. Wait. Back up. That was the vital life lesson I reaped from *The Karate Kid*. Still important advice, but not relevant here. After having fully briefed myself, via the internet, about how the babies would be extracted via C-section, I felt fairly confident about my own birthing experience. That is to say, I was ready for the Chipotle style of delivery. Wheel me in, I'll tell you what I can afford, and you hand me back a baby wrapped up like a burrito. No onions. Corona with a lime after, please.

Keeping to my strict expectations of life, nothing went as planned. Come to think of it, the only thing I can recall going as planned in my twenty-eight years on this planet was the one time I wore a thong to avoid panty lines, and retrieved it the next day using only my powers of deduction and a steady hand. But I'm digressing to places you're already actively avoiding in your mind's eye, so let's move on.

I couldn't have known everything that would happen after I put on that open-backed gown, settled into my bed, and let the nurse begin inserting the IV, a process which left Husband white as a sheet and asking if it was normal for the nurse to have a couple tries at it.

"Does blood on the floor count as success?" he asked.

I winked at him. "Of course. It's also a great way to let everyone know this is my room because I've already bled in here today." I squinted at the floor. "I can write my name if you want."

Shortly after I was attacked by the needle-wielding nurse, another doctor stopped in to check on me. "Well, good to see you're settling in. I spoke with your OB and she said she'd like to do the surgery first thing in the morning. So get something to eat and relax. We'll come prep you first thing in the morning."

With my hairy legs curled up under the covers I said, "Sounds good. Nothing I like better than a good, slightly dangerous, but intensely regulated medical procedure to start my morning. But, you say I can eat?"

He smiled. "Absolutely. Have some dinner and we'll be back to get you around five in the morning."

"And I can eat because I'm not having surgery until tomorrow?"

"Not until tomorrow."

"That's good because I wasn't supposed to eat before surgery."

"Not until tomorrow, Mrs. Kellerman."

"Tomorrow?"

"Tomorrow."

I was glad I'd been reassured so thoroughly because it gave me a chance to choke on the last of my pasta salad when the doctor came back in. "Your OB just called. She wants to deliver the babies now. Your blood pressure is through the roof."

I set down my fork and stared at him. "That's funny because I thought it was just fine until you came in and told me you want to open me up like a can of sardines in the next few minutes or so. Did you tell her I just ate?"

He busied himself with wires and tubes. "Don't worry, we have a drug for that."

"Quaaludes?"

"It'll keep you from getting sick since you just ate."

"Is that what you're putting in my IV right now?"

"Yes."

"The stuff that's making me shake and see flying monkeys do the Charleston as they come out of that bedpan?"

"Yes."

"Oh, good. For a second there, I thought you were going to tell me something I didn't want to hear. Lucky for you, I love bad news dressed up as mass confusion, wrapped up in a side of drug-induced haze." I saluted the room. "All right, let's move out. And make sure all of those monkeys are out of my bedpan by the time I get back. That can't be sanitary. This is a hospital, not a zoo, people."

I watched as Husband disappeared from sight and the gurney propelled me towards I had no idea what. The only thing that was clear was the inkling that there were about two gallons worth of drugs coursing through my veins and no one would let me have any water. Ten minutes prior, I hadn't needed water, nor ever been a huge water fan. Now, there were people on walkabouts in the Mojave Desert who didn't care for an Evian as much as I did. I would've sold a spare kidney to the first person with one hand out and a Brita pitcher in the other. How many times I asked isn't quite clear.

"Can I have some water?"

"No."

"Some crushed ice?"

"No."

"A Fresca?"

But by the time it dawned on me I wasn't ever getting any liquid to drink ever again, I'd already been wheeled into a three-ring circus complete with nurses working as hard as a road crew laying asphalt through the rainforest.

"Roll her on three, ladies. And mind those calves. We don't need a third cankle-related death in a month."

"But, Jackie, this one's so wide."

"That's fine, Hilda. Go ahead and bring out the front-end loader and an extra shovel."

All around me, bodies moved in no particular pattern I could figure out. It wasn't until I realized I was in an upright position that I fully began to comprehend the words.

"Hold still so I can insert the needle."

Needle? Needle? What needle? The doctor hadn't said anything about a needle. No, the hospital pamphlet had clearly shown a man who emerged with a set of pan-pipes and lulled me to sleep while the doctors extracted the babies. Hadn't it? What's the point of handing out informational packets if you're just going to stab me when we finally get down to brass tacks?

And yet, a man's voice behind me was clearly saying, "Ma'am, I'll need you to hold very still if I'm going to get your spinal block in correctly."

Mimicking a giant sloth, I leaned forward and wrapped myself around one of the nurses. "Oh, I'm sorry. I'm sure you always hold still for all of yours. How many children have you given birth to? Judging by your age and the fact that you're a man, I'd say it's probably around zero. I'm guessing you just took this job because the Harpooning Whales 101 intro class in college was already full of freshmen and seniors just dying to get that last credit so they could graduate and not get an empty diploma case like I did, with a note saying 'Nice try.' Oh, and the needle's only as big around as a straw from Sonic? By all means, let me bite down on this leather strap and let you get to work."

Fire up my spine. Still no water. And the sensation of having zero sensation. It was all so pleasant, the only way I could express my gratitude was to blink twice and pray the second act consisted of me trying to birth the babies myself while everyone laughed and took bets on how well I could wield a scalpel without the use of my arms.

"It's a good thing she had that fluoride treatment last time she was at the dentist, Bob. She's gonna need strong enamel to grip the knife and make a straight first incision."

"Agreed, Steve. Let's see how she does."

Up to this point, Husband hadn't been in the room. Consequently, when they finally admitted him, dressed in a sterile jump suit and stylish hairnet, I couldn't help but bring him up to speed.

"I can't feel my body."

He smiled. "I know."

One of the doctors piped up. "Okay, we're going to cut you a little bit to make sure you can't feel anything and that the anesthesia's doing its job."

I nodded and gave a light grunt of approval. Nothing says "we hope we gave you the right dosage" like being shanked with a steak knife.

"You feel that?"

I tried shaking my head. "No, and I gotta say I love the helpless feeling that all eight of you down there being able to see my exposed bottom half gives me. Makes a girl feel like she's got the whole world wrapped up in brown paper and tucked neatly in her pocket like dime-store candy."

"All right, Mrs. Kellerman. We're going to get started. You'll feel a little bit of pressure when we pull the babies out, but that should be all."

The next few moments were pretty hazy. I know there were people moving. I know I felt like the shark in *Jaws* who gets hauled on shore, gutted, and loses his license plate on the dock, but the only thing I concretely remember was the doctor saying, "It's a boy," and then, "It's a little girl."

Soon after, a nurse was holding something up for me

to kiss it, and it certainly looked like a burrito, a cotton-wrapped, beanie-wearing burrito. Soon after there was another red, chubby-faced person demanding it be kissed for all its efforts. And I'll readily admit they both looked less than pleased to have been dragged out of their sauna and into the equivalent of nuclear winter.

I can't say I blamed them. It must be horrifying to spend nine months warm and happy, only to be pulled out by strangers, shoved in the face of some woman who looks like a drug addict in a shower cap, and told, "This is the person who'll be raising you for the next eighteen years. She's hooked up to a catheter so she doesn't pee herself, and she keeps staring at you because she's high as a kite. But deep down, know that, somehow, she knows and loves you."

Luckily, the twins didn't have to think for long on the possibility they were being condemned to life in a crack house. Whisked away to be bathed and snuggled, the babies exited while I lay like a tanned dear carcass and had myself sewn up. Drug-induced haze puts this process at, roughly, eight hours. Drug-induced haze also caused me to start mumbling, "I'm so skinny," as I was wheeled back to my room. For anyone who's never given birth, pregnant women aren't skinny after they have a baby, but if they're on drugs, they feel like it, so the proper course of action, if a post-op pregnant woman starts screaming in front of you, "I'm so skinny," while trying to high five her own face, is to nod and start walking in the other direction. Preferably, try to go buy her some Jell-O in the cafeteria. If she's eating Jell-O, she won't notice how seriously cracked out she is and the fact that she only looks six months pregnant, instead of nine.

Husband did a great job of making me feel good when I made it back to the room. I beamed at him through the medication as they hooked me back up to urine-catching equipment.

"I'm so much smaller. Can you tell?"

"Actually, you look about the same."

Groggily, I looked around for the button to call the nurse, to have my better half removed from the room and someone who would lie to me put in his place. But as I poked at the controls, the world started spinning, and, as faceless people began filing into my room to see how I was and what our children looked like, I slipped out of consciousness and off to a place where I was instantly back in a bikini and my stomach didn't hit me in the face when I went to do a keg stand.

Postpartum
The Fun Never Stops

When people talk about childbirth, it's usually conversation wrapped in fuzzy blankets and size zero UGG boots. Women will ooh and aah about just getting the baby out and how tiring it is to be up all night. They'll say things like, "Just sleep when the baby sleeps," or, "It took nine months to get the baby weight on. It'll take nine to get it off." I was subjected to a lot of this type of jive before the twins were born. I ate it up with a spoon. In fact, if someone started giving me advice, I'd hold up my hand and say, "Let me just get out my spoon, so I can eat up everything you're saying. I don't want to miss one single bite. Why are you still talking? I told you I have to go find my spoon. It's these darn hobo bags. Can't find anything." I saved that useless spoon, dipped it in silver, and now use it to scrape all that gross stuff off the back of the toilet that one can never really get to.

The spoon deserves it. The spoon was an idiot. The spoon didn't bother to do any real, in-depth research about what happens after that cherub flies out of the secret trapdoor and someone wraps her or him in a toasty swaddling blanket, hands the bundle over, and says, "That'll be twenty thousand dollars, please." No, there are other ugly secrets that every other mother in the world keeps from you. Not because they don't care, but because nature programs this into anyone who's given birth, to block out any and all memory of the weirdness that can occur after delivery.

Oh, you won't sleep, my friends. In fact, I hold firm to the belief that there are Navy SEALs who would weep like small children if they went through that kind of sleep deprivation. In fact, by the second week that I'd been on my own with the twins, I was reporting to the refrigerator at two in the morning. "Sir, permission to go play in traffic, sir."

But there are other things besides the lack of sleep that no one ever mentions, like...

Post-partum bleeding: No one told me the first six weeks after delivery would be six weeks I'd need to avoid the tracking instincts of all brown bears and mountain lions. Or if I received the J. Crew catalog filled with white spring pants, I should probably roll it into a tube and use it as a pirate spy glass instead. "Arrr, Captain. I think she may be bleeding to death and will probably have to leave the children for her husband and society to raise."

Bloat: The first night home with the twins, I went upstairs to take a shower. Once I'd managed to hoist my broken body into the tub and turn the water on, I developed what I'm sure is known among respected members of the medical world as "inflatable foam toys in a pool syndrome." Where I'd once been a somewhat smaller, vacuum-sealed-and-dehydrated sponge dinosaur, nature decided to step in and make sure I was three times that size once I exited the shower. While the hot water coursed over me, instead of losing fluid, I gained half a ton, and waddled back downstairs looking like a little kid who'd just proudly proclaimed, "I ate all the things, ever." So for the ladies who will have babies in the near future, remember; bloating takes one to three weeks to get rid of, but most liquor stores are open until 11 pm.

Crying: I was back to more crying than I'd thought possible. I cried because I was tired, because my hair was a mess, because someone had decided to seal small foods into packages and I didn't have the mental focus to get a Twinkie out of its wrapper. I also cried because crying felt good.

"Are you okay? Are you going to be crying forever?" Husband asked.

"Probably."

"Good to know."

Don't ever let anyone tell you that you shouldn't cry. Let it all out. Pat yourself on the back. Find a baby seal to cuddle or five-toed fuzzy socks to wear—anything that makes you happy. If someone says you shouldn't be crying, feel free to find a watermelon and shove it up their nose. Then you'll both be crying and they can make delicious fruit salad afterwards.

The Pouch: First of all, I'd like to mention I'm drafting a petition to have any and all celebrities banned from talking about their birth experiences or post-partum recovery. I'm looking at you, Gwyneth Paltrow. Reading a famous person's account of how they got their "body back!" is quite a bit like reading a Grimm's fairy tale, except there aren't any dragons and Cinderella is a lying harlot.

The fact of the matter is there's a huge difference between when a normal woman gives birth and when a size zero supermodel orders a C-section/tummy tuck combo. She'll order fries on the side as a decorative garnish, but we all know she won't eat them. The supermodel will be rolled from the operating room, coasted directly to her trainer, and be fed lettuce through her IV. When she steps out of the hospital, she'll be as svelte as she was nine months before.

You, I, and the rest of the planet are left with what's affectionately still known to me as "The Pouch." The Pouch is capitalized because it might as well be a proper noun for how long many of us will have to carry it. It is the earliest ancestor of the fanny pack, but is unable to hold lip gloss or New Kids on the Block tickets. The only thing it can hold is nothing. The thing can't even hold itself in. The good news is, when dragging on the ground, it picks up spare dust and leaves floors with an impeccable sheen. No matter how hard one works out, it will always be there, reminding one that she is no longer a child but a woman with a pouch.

Disregarding all supermodels and actresses who've had their pouches removed, there are also some women who, magically, never receive the pouch. When I run into one of these anomalies, I find the best way to deal with the situation is to throw holy water on her and run as fast as possible the other way. The probability of her being immortal is high, which means she can also make it all the way through a Pilates DVD without needing to call the dog over and convince him to dial 911 with his jowls. Before she takes what's left of your soul, hike up your control-top yoga pants, squash your pouch into something as aerodynamic as possible, and run, my friends.

THE END

...or is it?

Acknowledgments

This book would not exist without all the lovely and beautiful people who made it a reality.

Husband. You know who you are. Thank you for making me sit down and write every night, even when I didn't feel like it. You are my best friend, and I love you.

Butch, Sundance, and Doc. Thank you for being adorable, happy and putting up with your mother. I love you all so much. Now, get off the cabinets.

My wonderful parents, brothers and sisters.

Sarah E. Holroyd. You edited this book within an inch of its life, and I'm truly grateful. Thank you for teaching me where elephants live.

Scarlett Rugers. You are a mastermind of design and the most patient person in the world. Thank you for answering my unending, ridiculous questions.

Robyn Welling. Thank you for the genius that is the backcopy of this book.

All the patient friends who took time out of their busy schedules to read and critique this book. You're my heroes.

The HBU. For your awesome support.

And a special thank you to Aileen. Without you, this book wouldn't have its title. Only you would let me repeatedly shout, "Cankle!" at you and still take me seriously.

10260288R00132

Made in the USA
San Bernardino, CA
10 April 2014